Lara Hogan

Demystifying Public Speaking

ISBN: 979-8-218-49672-2

10 9 8 7 6 5 4 3

Table of Contents

Foreword

IMAGINE IT: standing alone, up on a stage, bright lights in your eyes, a sea (or even a minor lake) of faces turned toward you, waiting for you to speak.

Did that scenario send you into a panic?

Then this book is for you.

Did that scenario hold no particular terror, because you're completely uninterested in being a public speaker?

Then this book is *still* for you.

Unless you're planning on a lifetime of hermitism—and trust me when I say I understand the appeal—you'll probably have to speak in public. Many times, even: presenting an idea to your team at work, giving a project overview to the top management, or trying to convince a group of colleagues to choose one course of action over another. Those count as public speaking, every bit as much as standing onstage for an hour. And the tips and techniques Lara Hogan shares in this book apply to both situations.

There's power in understanding this: if you've always wanted to be a public speaker, up onstage sharing what you know, but are too terrified to try it, realize that you've been speaking in public for years and years. The difference between doing it in a conference room and doing it in an assembly hall is mostly one of audiovisual support. They're different points on a spectrum, but it's the same spectrum.

Whether you want to contribute your voice in small groups at work or in front of crowds at a big event, this book can help you speak more clearly and confidently. We all have something to contribute. We all have a unique perspective and insights that are new to other people. By hearing one another's stories, we all advance.

We're eagerly waiting to hear yours.

—Eric Meyer

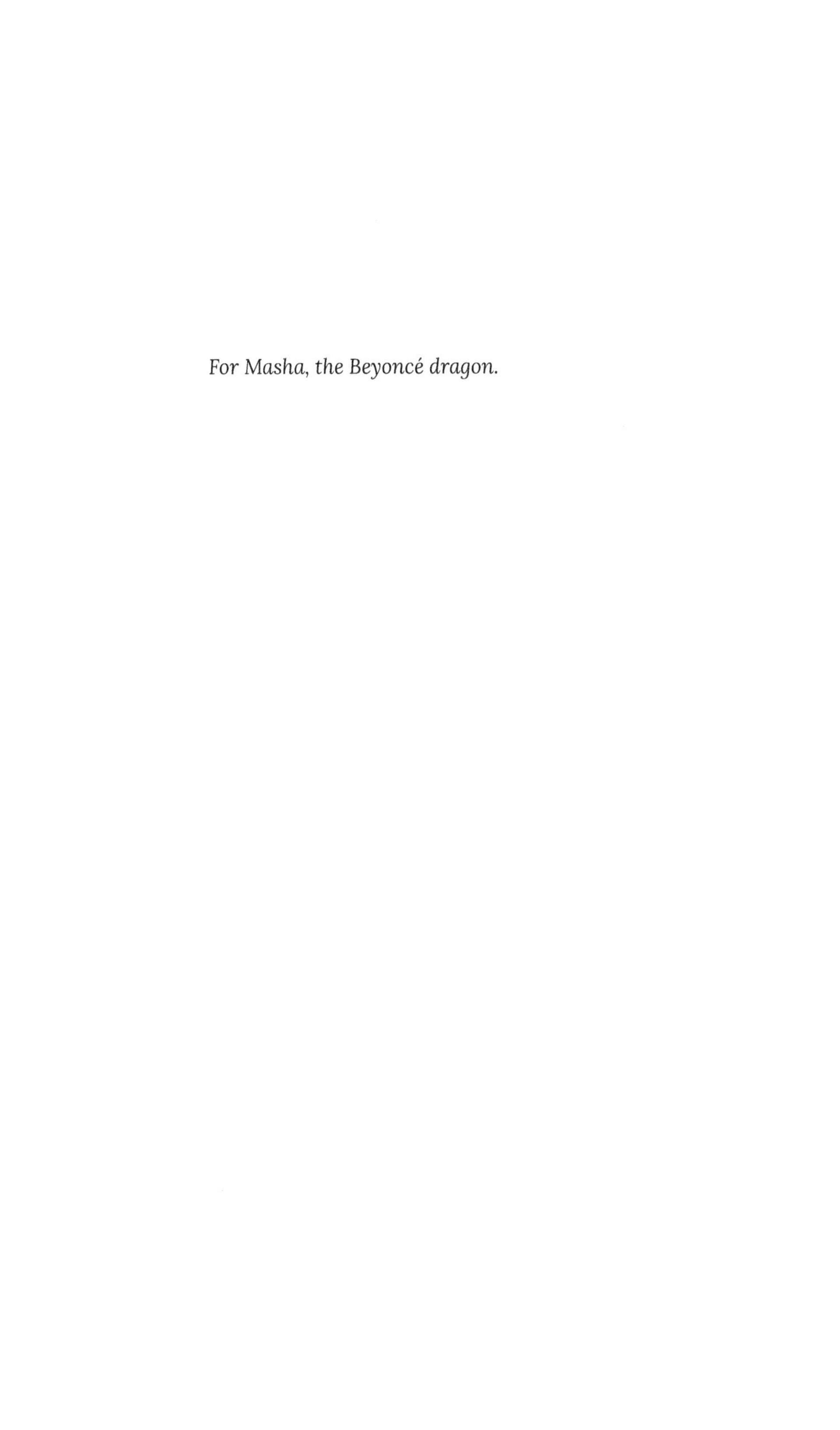

For Masha, the Beyoncé dragon.

Introduction

MY FIRST CONFERENCE TALK was a keynote—by accident.

I'd prepared a deeply technical talk on web performance, heavy on the "how" of image and markup optimizations. I'd designed and timed my slides, gathered feedback from coworkers, and practiced over and over. I was nervous about going onstage and having a spotlight shining on me, but I was confident my information was accurate and helpful to a technical audience.

Days before the conference, I took a look at the schedule and realized I was slotted into the opening talk—the keynote, a spot intended to inspire a much more general audience than the one I'd planned on. Whoops. I tried to revamp my slides to be more approachable and to end with a bigger kick.

But that was just the first red flag. On the day of the conference, I stood by the side of the stage and braced myself for that spotlight. As the emcee introduced me to the crowd of 400, I heard a bio that wasn't...mine. As the career highlights of not-me sank in, I realized the organizers thought I was someone else. I'm still not sure who they had meant to invite, or who they thought I was, but there was definitely a mistake.

The mess escalated. The organizers couldn't provide water to the speakers, having gotten in a fight with the venue's event management company. They forgot to turn the lights down, and my white-text, black-background slides became unreadable. I was thrown off too: during Q&A, I thought one person was joking with their question, so I laughed. They weren't, and my reply went over like a lead balloon.

It wasn't my best talk. But I went on to get comfortable giving dozens more, in many different countries before thousands of people.

Being onstage is an incredibly vulnerable act. It's risky. And, let's face it, public speaking is *weird*: we can't really practice it without doing it—we don't really have a way to slowly dip our toes in. More likely, we take the plunge into the spotlight, to be ourselves in a way people might not like.

What if I mess up? What if they don't like what I have to say? What if they disagree, or worse, what if they don't like me?

We *all* have fears about public speaking. That's okay! Luckily, we also have plenty of resources to draw on that focus on how to write and deliver a great talk (you can find some picks in the Resources section). With this book, though, I want to reassure you. Consider this an introduction to getting *comfortable* with public speaking. Because you can do it. If I survived that bananas first keynote and kept practicing and getting better, you can too.

I want to help you learn about what *you* bring to public speaking: your expertise, your style, your fears, your strengths. Each chapter includes tips and techniques (from others' experiences as well as my own) to ease you into different aspects of giving a talk. I want to help you figure out what makes you tick, gain more confidence, and maybe even have some fun when you're up onstage.

I hope you'll feel more prepared and excited to give talks. Most important, I hope this book helps you find ways to be yourself, rather than hew to any public speaking "rules" or givens. We desperately need more diverse voices in this industry speaking up and sharing their knowledge. I can't wait to see what you do—I can't wait for the rest of us to listen and learn from you.

CHAPTER ONE

Step zero

Before you near the stage, before you write the talk, before you even pick a topic, take time to get comfortable with the idea of giving a talk.

You're reading this because something about public speaking makes your palms sweat. You aren't alone; when I created an anonymous survey and asked, "What's your biggest fear about public speaking?" I received over 300 replies. Though the fears all revolved around being vulnerable in front of a large group of people, I was surprised how widely the responses ranged.

See for yourself—I've grouped a handful of replies to illustrate the spectrum of fears.

- **People are worried about their voices:**
  - "The sound or pitch of my own voice."
  - "Voice cracking up—I forget to breathe from the diaphragm and come across sounding nervous and uninformed."

- "Forgetting or skipping over what I want to say, heart racing (and getting out of breath quicker), getting tongue-tied."
- **People are worried about their bodies:**
  - "Being judged for being fat, not on my presentation content."
  - "In middle school I got something in my eye during a class presentation, and my eyes would not stop watering. I'm terrified it will happen again."
  - "Needing to pee during the speech!"
  - "Falling on stage."
  - "People judging my appearance, whether I'm dressed appropriately."
- **People are worried about technical or wardrobe malfunctions:**
  - "Problems connecting laptop to projector."
  - "Making stupid coding mistakes during live coding."
  - "Open pants zipper (because it's happened)."
- **People are worried about being wrong and being challenged:**
  - "Elegantly explaining something that is actually wrong."
  - "Showing that I'm ignorant about something I thought I was knowledgeable about."
  - "Getting a question I can't even begin to answer."
  - "Being wrong and being called out on stage during Q&A."
  - "Getting heckled."
  - "Vocal skeptics or doubters."
- **People are worried about their performance:**
  - "Not being impressive enough."
  - "That everything I say becomes so messy anyone can refute it."
  - "Since I'm not a native English speaker, my biggest fear is not making any sense when speaking."
  - "That no one learns anything, and the audience is starkly aware of it."
  - "Being exposed for the fraud I have always felt like."

Phew. Given the potential for these moments of total—human—disaster, why should we even bother embarking on this journey toward the stage?

To start, public speaking (or put another way, broadcasting your abilities and knowledge) has definite career benefits. You grow your network by meeting attendees and other speakers, and you gain documented leadership experience in your subject area. People looking to hire, collaborate with, or fund someone with your topic expertise will be able to find you, see proof of your work, and have a sense of the new perspective you'll bring to future projects.

Those professional benefits are huge—but in my experience, the personal benefits are even more substantial. Giving a talk grows so many skill sets: crafting a succinct way to share information, reading an audience, and eloquently handling an adrenaline-heavy moment. You'll prove something to yourself by overcoming a major fear, and you should take pride in knowing you taught a large group of people something new that will hopefully make their work or lives easier. Public speaking experience boosts a lot of knock-on benefits too, like a stronger visa application or more confidence in your everyday spotlight moments, like a standup meeting, code review, design critique, or other project presentations.

No matter the impetus, trying your hand at public speaking is a brave act. While it's a different challenge for everyone, we do have a few tools to help tackle our fears.

Flip that fear around

First, give yourself permission to be anxious. Even renowned speaker and industry veteran Eric Meyer still gets nervous giving talks, as detailed in his article "The Stages of Fear":

> *A hundred public talks or more, and it's still not easy. I'm not sure it ever will be easy. I'm not sure it ever should be easy. [...] Every speaker I know feels pretty much exactly the same. We don't all get the same nervous tics, but we all get nervous. We struggle with our fears and doubts. We all feel like we have no idea what we're*

Being nervous is totally normal. Consider what you're juggling: sharing information, entertaining the audience, and guessing (or worrying over) how you're being perceived. Keep in mind, though, being nervous is not a sign you'll do poorly. Public speaking isn't an everyday context, and you may still get butterflies even as you gain experience and improve your speaking game.

But if you can't coolly eliminate all your fears and nerves like some stoic robot, what *can* you do? One tactic to try is reframing your anxiety in a positive or motivating way, as designer Lea Alcantara suggests:

> *Instead of worrying, flip your perception of nerves as an indication you care as opposed to dread of failure. There is no shame in caring deeply about a subject and what people think about your talk. (http://ladiesintech.com/self-fulfilling-prophecy/)*

Caring feels a lot more approachable than dreading failure, and it gives you a way through: use your body's natural reaction to stress to improve your talk. Invest that energy into more research of your topic, more practice, and more feedback-gathering—all acts within your control. Let your nerves become part of the process—or try accepting that—and just maybe, in time, they'll feel more useful than disastrous.

What makes you tick?

To flip your fears into motivations, let's dip into what makes you tick. Understanding who you are will help you determine where to invest that extra energy as you make your way toward the stage. Once you begin to name what scares you, what comforts you, and what drives you, you'll be able to home in on which talk format, topic, venue type, and preparation style will calm those fears and build your excitement.

To get you started, think through these:

- What makes you most *excited* when you think about public speaking? What do you want to get out of it?
- What makes you most *nervous* when you think about public speaking? What scenarios do you want to avoid?
- What size audience do you think you might be most comfortable speaking to? Why?
- Whose feedback matters most to you on your talk or presentation style?
- What would you want people to take away from your talk?
- What do you want to happen for you or your career after your talk? (Examples: someone offers you your dream project, someone you admire asks for your advice, people shower you with praise, you get right back to work, etc.)

That's a lot of introspection, but it's worth it. As we move through this book, we'll go through the varied paths and aspects of public speaking, and your answers will guide you to the right fit for you. For instance, if you're afraid of seeing a sea of strange faces before you, maybe a smaller meetup is the best venue to get in some practice. If you're afraid of saying something patently false onstage, then pick a topic like a case study from your work that you know inside and out, and practice your Q&A session with friends who can help you fact-check your content. Or, if you're excited to teach people skills they can immediately put into practice, opt for a workshop format and give hands-on help to folks. Whatever your goals and style, you can find a speaking opportunity that resonates with you.

Move beyond the "rules"

You've heard the adages: don't say "um," don't say "uh." Excise "like" with extreme prejudice. Don't use bullets on your slides. Never, ever read from your notes. Some folks have an archetype of what a great speaker sounds like, or an audience size that feels real, or this idea you need to give a deeply technical or novel talk for it to count.

But you know what? If I can say one thing in this book about giving talks, it's *do what works for you*. Truly.

Of course, it's hard to move past the impulse to embrace rules—it's reassuring to think we have a straightforward map to success. We try to mimic speakers who capture our attention or those whom our peers praise. We hold up examples of "ideal" presentation styles, and we instruct new speakers to follow suit. We *see* a lot of the same people, and we can't help but absorb a lot of the same opinions on what a good speaker looks like or sounds like.

Just because we've built a system, it doesn't mean it's right. What we need to see represented onstage is a spectrum of speakers with different insights and ways to teach us about them. Your voice is valuable, and your own. If you choose to share it, we will all certainly be the better for it.

Public speaking is a journey that, like any other, involves practice and time to make you feel comfortable and successful. Take heart from Tiffani Jones Brown:

> *The worst case scenario is your talk flops—in which case you'll be stronger for it. The likelier scenario is you'll give a couple decent talks, followed by better ones, followed by even better ones, until you give one that really makes a difference. (http://ladiesintech. com/why-i-speak/)*

I don't want to set out any rules in this book—forget them. What I do hope is to help you forge your own path, so you make your way to that talk that makes a difference. Let's get started.

CHAPTER TWO

Choosing a topic

WHAT YOU CHOOSE TO FOCUS ON in your talk is the product of many things: the content that inspires you, the level of depth you're comfortable sharing, and what you learn as you take your topic for a test spin with others.

No perfect order of operations exists to picking your talk topic. You might've already found a venue to speak at (which we get to in the next chapter), one with its own guidelines on format or topic. Or, maybe you're starting from scratch, and you're looking for some parameters to make initial brainstorming sessions as productive as possible. At the end of the day, what we're aiming for is a fruitful topic you feel really comfortable speaking about.

101 is okay!

This is a praise song for "intro to ABC" talks: if you're feeling anxious about blowing minds or going deep on a particular topic, stick to the basics.

My early inspiration came from introducing my projects to coworkers. At my job, I focused on web performance and ways to clean up site templates to make everything load faster for our users. People would ask, "How did you save so many image bytes?" I'd break down the steps, along with the pros and pitfalls of implementing each fix.

I trotted out this presentation to more teams and shared what I learned on the company blog. By then, I could also point to huge wins from existing work as examples, and I'd reframe the topic to land best with each team—focusing on how our site speed compared to competitors' when presenting to the marketing team, or how many milliseconds we'd shaved off when presenting to developers. Through writing and having these conversations, I grew more comfortable both building a narrative around my work and sharing it.

And that's a talk! Your topic doesn't have to be the most inspiring, thought-leading idea in the universe. 101 talks are a terrific way to gain practice: the information often applies to a wider spectrum of job roles (aka more people wanting to learn), they are versatile and can be tweaked per audience, and conferences are generally eager for them. Plus, you have a built-in test audience through your work (if you're in-house) or with potential clients (if you're freelancing).

So don't discount intro-level talks. Even though I've branched out into speaking on deeper, more technical topics, I still think audiences get the *most* out of my intro-level talks, because the content is entirely new to them. They're super-engaged during Q&A, and they highly rate my talks after the conference concludes.

Brainstorm from your work

Another way to finding your topic: look no farther than your own desk (or laptop). What do you spend lots of your day thinking about or working on?

Large projects are great sources of inspiration, because they feature so many facets you could shine up for a talk. No matter what facet you choose (tools! human stuff! problem solving!), your future audience has felt its challenges.

Maybe you want to give a how-to on the language you learned to code a project, or walk through how you chose one tool over others. Maybe your project received feedback from stakeholders late in the game, and you want to share how you'll get buy-in earlier next time. Or you might talk about initial bottlenecks, like deciding on and coordinating an approach that worked for all the teams involved.

Each of these possible topics contains a relatable story, an inspiration, a demonstration, or a new approach for someone in your audience. But which? To get your mind whirring, let's check out a few facets of the challenges in your meaty project.

Get to the root of the challenge

Examine your biggest project hurdle, and ask: Was the hardest part people-related or deliverables-related? This can help you understand who your primary audience might be, or what format (a how-to, a workshop, even a panel) best fits. For instance, talks about people and culture can apply to a broader audience, with varying roles or levels of experience. A deliverables-driven talk heavy on technical specifics might match a more niche event—or, you could take a 101-level approach to the technical bits to attract a more general audience.

Share your process

Another approach is to examine the entire timeline, not just how you overcame a challenge. Was the roadblock a surprise? How could you reduce the likelihood of it happening in the future? Did it affect others, and how did you work with them or communicate the problem? Process talks like these are nice starter topics, because they have a natural story arc (encountering a problem, working through it, achieving results, reexamining initial assumptions), and people tend to be curious about how others do their work.

Reassess your solution

In hindsight, could you have chosen other, better approaches? What would you want to teach (or warn!) others, based on what you learned? Some of the best talks wrestle with mistakes or outright failure—they tend to be very relatable (aka human), and the stakes can make for a compelling setup.

How juicy is it?

While not a requirement, "juiciness" is another angle to consider as you vet your topic (a good hook also helps your odds in the talk submissions process). Sample juicy aspects and scenarios include:

- **Timeliness/newness:** Is this technology or approach to your work the kind that's hotly debated online? Are you providing new data on how Tool XYZ is a much better fit than Tool ABC in certain conditions?
- **Cultural complexity:** Were you tasked with making big decisions that were fairly political, like requiring a client to overhaul their design workflows, or buy into a mobile strategy for the first time?
- **Going against the grain:** Were the lessons you learned during the work counterintuitive or contrary to best practices? Would your solution—while efficient and effective—flabbergast some folks?

Picking a topic that has some drama (and balancing that with solid takeaways) helps keep an audience engaged throughout your talk.

Size up your topic

You have a few contenders—now size them up to see if they have enough weight to carry an entire talk. Check your topic's potential by naming concrete takeaways, identifying a story structure, and testing your topic against constraints like talk format or time slot.

Focus on takeaways

The takeaways matter the most to your audience. Often, if an audience member is employed by a company, they'll need to make a case to their manager to attend an event. Weekday events like conferences want to make it easy to "sell" a boss on the expense and time away from the office, so they'll construct a lineup of talks to help people be better coworkers and employees. List the immediately actionable lessons you could share from your topic. What could the audience implement when they're back at their desk? How can you frame your topic to inspire people to try that work? Would those benefits appeal to a higher-up sending an employee to see your talk?

You also want your audience to get a solid grasp on any context they need to understand your points. Will they have enough prerequisite knowledge, or will you need to spend time teeing up your topic?

Think about how you'll deliver those takeaways. Don't worry about nailing down a solid outline or full structure now (we'll talk about writing the talk in Chapter 4). Do explore how each takeaway might lead to the next (maybe you opt for a linear story arc, with a clear beginning, middle, and end) or how they fit together (maybe you choose a more thematic approach).

Consider constraints

If you already have sights on an event, adopt its format or time slot and go from there. For example, if you're sharing a case study or demo, sketch out the project challenge or what steps to showcase. If you're crafting a workshop or tutorial, note what skill or deliverable you'd like attendees to leave with, which examples to present, or how you'd like to divide the time (lecture versus small groups versus hands-on practice).

Consider how long it might take to cover your topic. Minutes? Hours? (Speaking opportunities run the gamut!) How much time do you need to dedicate to sharing prerequisite context before moving onto actionable lessons? Jot down an outline, using one index card per thought, and see how many cards you need to introduce and support your thesis statement. If you're adding more cards that go on a long tangent, or if it takes a lot of time to lay the groundwork, you may need to revisit your original angle.

Otherwise, if your topic sails through these checks—clear arc, strong takeaways, appropriate fit for your format or time—you're ready to level up and get to workshopping.

Take your topic for a test spin

Hooray! You've got an angle on a topic you believe has legs. But before you dive into writing, take your topic for a test run—make sure it resonates with *others*.

My favorite way to vet a potential topic is to write about it. Writing helps me figure out which of my thoughts I really mean—or which ones lead to ideas I can build on. (This is great for experimenting.) Sharing what you've written—to a group of friends via email, or to internet strangers via published article or blog post—can give you insight into what ideas or approaches to a topic resonate best, which in turn helps you learn more about how to present the information.

I've been most confident presenting content I've written about numerous times. Because I've already articulated my thought process and defended my reasoning in text, I don't worry as much about whether what I'm saying makes sense to other people. From my public posts, I'm able to iterate on how I communicate my points by responding to comments on the article, questions on Twitter, or feedback from my coworkers. Shaping a talk becomes an everyday process—I can take my time developing my future topics and share them as I feel comfortable.

Or maybe you learn best by doing: try giving a mini-presentation. Again, you might start with friends or colleagues. Or go for an event with more structure. For example, at an Ignite Talk, a speaker has five minutes total to explain their subject while using twenty slides that automatically advance in fifteen-second internals (http://www.ignitetalks.io/). Sticking to such requirements (a lot of information in a very short time) could help you uncover the most important aspects of your topic. As with writing, giving a mini-talk also offers the opportunity to receive early feedback. I've gotten great questions during Q&A that made me realize I should include content on how to get other people to care about site speed; this shaped my performance talk for the better.

The paradox of topic choice is real. It can be tough to believe you know enough on a particular topic to speak on it; it can also be tough to narrow things down to the *one* thing you want to present on. Take time to think through your topic, and see what feels the most fruitful for you and your potential audience.

CHAPTER THREE

Finding a venue

FROM SPEAKING TO COWORKERS at your company to speaking to strangers at another company, from speaking to a dozen people at a meetup to speaking to a hundred—or a thousand—at a conference, the right venue (or venues!) exists for you. I promise. Some may feel high-stakes, others low.

Let's look at three public speaking venues to help you find your fit: educational lunches, meetups, and conferences.

Lunch and learns

A typical "brown-bag lunch" or "lunch and learn" is a meeting among coworkers, in which someone teaches a topic or skill. I love doing these mini events—they tend to be less formal and are more approachable (food helps). I also enjoy the smaller crowd and the opportunity to workshop a future talk in a trusted group.

Educational lunches (or meetings) aren't limited to your company; plenty of organizations bring in outside speakers. If you want to try out a more anonymous crowd (say, in prep for a conference), or you'd like some perspectives from a different company culture or process, reach out! See if you know someone who works there, who could put you in touch with the appropriate person. Ask if they'd like to host you for an hour to share your knowledge and answer questions.

The logistics of a lunch and learn can be a little tricky. Unlike conferences or meetups, these talks might not have a dedicated event organizer, so it's much more on you to coordinate what you need. Etsy product design lead Karyn Campbell, who routinely invites prominent designers to talk to Etsy's design team, cautions, "Oftentimes casual environments like meeting rooms aren't set up for other purposes." Plan ahead if you'll need to adjust seating or address A/V issues. (You might face a few technical bumps anyway—and it's okay! I've found it's helpful to field a variety of tech issues, as now I can enter pretty much any event setup and feel confident I'll work through it.)

If reveling in logistics is not your idea of a good time, look to those outside companies. If they host speakers often, they probably have a sense of their technical and timing requirements; ask them to confirm what you should bring. You'll likely need your own remote, handouts, or other auxiliary equipment.

Meetups

A meetup is akin to a smaller conference event, with a larger emphasis on networking and social time. Meetups are as diverse in style as conferences; some are very formal, others are low-key. Some meetups have a lone talk or no talks scheduled; others have a list of rotating speakers.

A meetup is an excellent way to grow your public speaking skills. For one, you'll have a mix of new and familiar faces in the room. It's also a great venue if your talk has a super-specific focus, as meetups tend to center on niches like "Android development" or "women in tech." Your audience will have a range of skill sets and experiences within that world—an ideal crowd to help you further develop and refine your ideas. (As a bonus: meetups are great for networking if you're hoping to find a new collaborator or gig, or recruit someone for your team!)

Meetups have a lot of positives, but the emphasis on networking time and the inclusion of alcohol can make it harder for some folks to participate. How do you know if a meetup is a good fit? Go see for yourself, and speak with other attendees (and know you can leave early if you don't feel comfortable). If you like the vibe, chat with the organizers about their goals, measures of success, and any pitching process.

Conferences

Conferences are the site of flop sweats, triumphs, and a check off the bucket list—what many people picture first when someone says "public speaking."

These events are put on by an organizer or group of organizers whose job is to find funding, attract attendees, craft a speaker lineup, organize audio and visual support, find a venue, and much more. In addition, the same or another group of people may vet proposals for talks.

You may have heard about single-track or multi-track conference types. A single-track event takes place in one room, where all attendees gather and hear all of the speakers in order. Everyone sees the same talks, so audience members don't have to spend energy choosing which ones to see or finding the correct room, and they have a more communal experience. A multi-track event has multiple rooms or spaces for concurrent talks. Attendees pick which talks they'd like to see, so they might be better prepared for learning (and more enthusiastic) about your particular topic.

In the next sections, I'll walk through what goes on behind the scenes at most conferences so that, armed with facts, we can decrease some of the unknowns around public speaking at this kind of event. Keep in mind it's tough to say whether you'll encounter any particular trait of a conference because they're all run so differently. But by illustrating the spectrum of conferences, I hope to help you figure out which aspects might feel like the right comfort zone for you.

Finding a conference

On your journey to landing your dream conference, let's start with a visualization. Think about your future talk: who do you picture in the audience?

Be as detailed as possible. What kinds of jobs do they have? Do they work in the same industry, like higher education or government—or do they have similar roles, like designers or developers? Do they belong to any professional groups? What blogs or magazines do they read? Who do they follow on Twitter? What meetups or conferences are they excited about?

Thinking about your ideal audience—and their interests—is one way to pinpoint your ideal speaking venue.

Further your research by asking your friends, coworkers, or other people in your target demographic about their real-life experiences. Can they think of a conference, meetup, or other venue where they enjoyed learning? Even better, can they recall an event where they enjoyed *speaking*?

Gather more inspiration from the site Lanyrd (http://lanyrd. com/), which amasses lists of events and their history, including location, topics, and past speakers. You might also try the newsletter Technically Speaking (http://www.techspeak.email/), which collects conferences currently soliciting proposals for new talks (also known as a CFP, or Call for Proposals). As you document your list of potential places to speak, note whether they have a CFP or other submissions process. If they have a proposal deadline, put a reminder on your calendar to submit!

Once you have your list, start narrowing the field. Here are a few questions I ask myself to see if an event would be a good fit.

What is the event's reputation?

Dig online and see what attendees have said. If this is the event's first year, scope out the organizers. Audience enthusiasm is a terrific sign, of course, but even better, see if people were inspired to take what speakers shared and change how they worked or thought about about a topic. You'll get a sense of what the audience responds to. If you know any past speakers, reach out and ask them how it went: what the audience was

like, how the event was run, and whether they'd recommend
it to other speakers.

How organized is the event?
What's the level of speaker support?

Is the event loosely organized with a more casual feel, or is it
highly structured with a more formal schedule? Or a mix?

This will help you figure out the level of work involved on
your end (including how much preparation you'll want to do)
and give you an idea of how much support the organizers
can offer you—which might be important if you have specific
logistics needs for travel, compensation, accessibility, food,
etc., or if you want early feedback on your presentation. For
example, !!Con, a conference for programmers, helps speakers
develop their talks. Maggie Zhou, a past !!Con organizer, told me:

> *[Event organizers] desperately want the conference to go well,
> and so are totally willing to help you the speaker in whatever way
> you need. So ask for help if you need it. For !!Con, we listened to
> people's talks ahead of time on video and in person, and talked
> people through expectations and setup, and would've been willing
> to do much more than that!*

While !!Con's collaborative approach might not always be
available, it doesn't hurt to ask. Coaching a speaker through
giving their first talk benefits both the speaker and the
conference, as it'll result in a better talk and a better experience
for the audience.

Introducing and supporting new speakers to the circuit
brings a more diverse array of voices and perspectives to our
industry. Which leads us to the next question.

How inclusive is the event?

Look at the speaker bios of past lineups. Some conferences have
been intentional about ensuring their speaker lineup is diverse,
such as inviting people from underrepresented communities or
using a CFP system that anonymizes submissions.

Consider safety concerns too. Look for conferences with a Code of Conduct, which outlines expectations for participants' behavior, resources to reach out to if anyone has concerns, and consequences for those who break the code. These guidelines have gained traction in our industry to help prevent harassment: racist, sexist, ableist, trans- or homophobic, or otherwise intolerant language; online hate mobs; threats of violence; sexual assault.

Codes of Conduct should provide clear rules for behavior *and* guidelines for their enforcement. Event organizers may emphasize to speakers that their content should adhere to the code; in addition, check that organizers have trained staff in the specific processes for handling inappropriate behavior and harassment at the conference or a related event. Seek out conferences that articulate the importance of safety for their speakers and attendees.

What's the level of expected socializing?

Conferences encourage a range of interaction with the audience and other speakers in the course of the event. I've seen organizers:

- host a Slack channel for attendee (and speaker!) camaraderie
- facilitate lunch table conversation topics, or assign speaker tables during meals, so attendees can congregate around topics that interest them and ask more questions
- host a happy hour or other social event for attendees, and require speakers to attend and speak to folks
- host a welcome dinner for speakers, so they can get to know one another and the organizers

Maybe structured social events (like happy hours) boost your spirits, or maybe you prefer solo downtime. Maybe both hold true. See how a conference might complement (or drain) your energy levels, so you can better plan. In recent years, conferences have offered activities that don't revolve around alcohol (like walking tours), and carved out quiet rooms for attendees and speakers. Some events have a separate speakers' lounge, so speakers can prepare or connect with one another in a quieter space. I also like to head for the "hallway track," informal places where attendees chat with one another about past sessions, follow-up questions, or their own company practices. I've found these conversations to be as valuable as the conference talks themselves.

Does the location pose travel or cultural concerns?

Consider concerns external to the conference too. For instance, I spoke to Juan Pablo Buriticá, who organizes a number of conferences in Colombia, on the importance of researching an event that takes place in another country:

> *Culturally, you may have plenty of differences on what to expect outside of the US. This may also have a bigger impact in underrepresented communities for several reasons. For example, I know of a speaker who decided to opt out of a conference due to a State Department assessment on the state of LGBT rights in Latin America.*

Take the time to understand cultural expectations. You might register with your consulate if you're headed abroad. Buriticá also suggests talking to event organizers or your employer (if possible) about safety and security while traveling.

Get in the door

You have two routes to speaking at an event: submitting a proposal or being invited. When you're starting out, or if you're switching gears to a new topic, you'll likely embark on the submissions track. Let's get excited about filling out some forms!

Submitting a proposal

Each conference has its set of questions about your talk content, format, and you, the speaker. Organizers use this information to figure out if you and your talk suit their event and audience. For example, a typical O'Reilly conference might ask for:

- The proposed title
- Both an elevator pitch and an extended description of the presentation
- The topics you'll cover
- A biography and headshot
- A video of the speaker giving a talk
- Any anticipated expenses, like travel reimbursement

Once the submissions are in, organizers cull them and decide what shape the conference should take, based on industry trends and key takeaways for the audience. Some conference organizers read all of the submissions themselves; others arrange panels to gain more diverse perspectives. As they consider contenders, organizers put themselves in their audience's shoes: what does that audience *want* to hear?

That's a question you should keep in mind as you create your pitch. Sarah Mei does a fantastic job exploring the sales aspects of writing a proposal in her article "What Your Conference Proposal Is Missing":

> People don't go to talks for the content. People go to talks because they think they'll become more badass. So help them out with that! Make it easy for them to imagine their newfound superpowers, and they'll match your level of excitement. (http://www.sarahmei.com/blog/2014/04/07/what-your-conference-proposal-is-missing/)

For more on writing proposals, hop to the Resources section. But let's back up and return to you. Have you ever looked at a CFP form for your dream event—the one that always has the best lineup and most fun participants—and chosen not to submit? If you said *yes*, you're in good company. Maybe you share some of the fears people noted in my public speaking survey:

- "I'm afraid I'll fail to tell people something new and interesting."
- "What if I choose a topic that's been done to death?"
- "No one would want to listen to me talk about anything."

Don't take yourself out of the running before the people organizing the event have had a chance to look at your proposal. It's literally their job to find talk topics that will be relevant and enticing to their audience; you can help their cause—and yours—by choosing conferences whose audience and focus lines up with yours.

If you're still a little unsure or plain stuck, get a second pair of eyes on your draft! Ask a colleague or friend to give feedback on questions like "Would this topic be helpful for this event's audience?" or "Is this the right level of depth for a proposal?"

Skipping the line

Once you're on the speaking circuit, you begin to get invited a *lot* more to give talks, rather than submitting a proposal through the normal channels.

I've received invites via Twitter direct messages, out-of-the-blue emails, and connections from trusted friends. Some invites include lots of information about the conference and what they hope I'll bring to it. Sometimes they include a list of other speakers who've confirmed their talks, as a way to convince me that I want to be on that roster.

An invite doesn't automatically mean you're in; some organizers extend invitations to *submit* an idea, while others ask you to give a particular kind of talk—which you might not want to do! Feel free to see if they would be interested in a different take.

For instance, as I've done a lot of web performance talks, organizers often invite me to present the same talk at their event. Some places will ask me to change the length of the talk (I can tell you it's rough to cram a 90-minute workshop into a 30-minute lecture!), and others ask for completely new material.

As ever, ask questions in turn. Event organizers want and need you to succeed—get their perspective before you submit your pitch. I'll check if they'd prefer a 101-level topic or more depth; or I'll see if they have any subject gaps in their lineup they'd like me to cover. Recently, I spoke at a conference that attracts more designers, so I refocused my performance talk to include design considerations on site speed. You want to go for something that feels good to present and is equally as fulfilling for your audience to hear.

You won't get invitations to every conference you want—and it's okay. Keep submitting, whether it's through a CFP or your network. The more practice you get with sending proposals, the more you can learn from the process and event organizers about what makes a winning pitch. Follow up with any rejections (we all get them!) to find out what wasn't quite the right fit, and see if that feedback applies to your next submission. Maybe it's as simple as "We already had three proposals on the same topic," or as helpful as "This wasn't the right technical depth for our audience." Learning and iterating is the key to each step toward the stage.

Locking it in

Excellent, you're in! The event organizers have given you an enthusiastic thumbs up, and you're ready to commit.

Negotiate your compensation

Compensation and arrangements vary *wildly*, and it's hard to get figures. Some conferences pay speakers an honorarium or flat fee. Some events cover travel and/or lodging; this coverage could top out at a certain dollar amount or vary depending on distance or other needs like childcare. Other conferences may simply cover the cost of your ticket to the conference itself.

When I was getting started, I asked events to cover travel and lodging, but I rarely received other compensation. Because I had a full-time, salaried job and didn't need to take vacation days to speak at the conference, this setup worked for me. I didn't know I *could* ask for a speaker fee, let alone negotiate other kinds of compensation like a per diem or upgraded flights. I was a rookie, but I've negotiated a lot more since.

I encourage you to ask to be adequately compensated for your time and hard work in giving audiences a good experience. What do you need to be able to speak at the event? You always have the option of talking to an organizer, and you *can* negotiate travel or childcare or more conference tickets. As you calculate your speaker fee, consider the real time it takes to create a talk—and factor in related expenses: any vacation days you'll need to take, meals during your trip, passport or visa fees, pet care, even new clothing.

One terrific place to start researching your compensation options is Who Pays Speakers? (http://whopays.techspeakers. info/), an anonymous survey that collects and shares information on speakers' compensation and event experiences. Another great resource is developer Jenn Lukas's take on calculating speaking fees (http://www.thenerdary.net/post/84544230452/a-formula-for-speaking-fees), which breaks down ways to translate the work of creating and giving a talk into numbers.

Negotiating compensation, especially as a newer speaker, can feel acutely uncomfortable. But remember, you're doing a job! Ask yourself what kind of compensation would make the experience worthwhile.

Review what you're agreeing to

Does the event have a contract? If they don't, consider drawing one. Typically a contract includes information on logistics, deliverables and deadlines, and compensation. Sally Jenkinson has shared her standard speaking contract online (https://gist. github.com/greywillfade/61bb24ebb2a240d8d3d3). She includes relevant details like a short bio for marketing materials, the name of her talk, and an agreement to be photographed.

Before you sign on the dotted line (after a thorough read-through), ask the organizers a few questions to ensure this opportunity is the right fit for you:

- **Audience size:** ask how many people they expect to attend and if the conference is single-track or multi-track. If it's a smaller conference and multi-track, you may be speaking to a very small room. Knowing the rough audience size can help you imagine what it'll be like when you're onstage, looking out at the crowd. See if this audience size feels right for your comfort zone.

- **Logistics:** ask about the space and broad logistics (like how early you can check your laptop setup, if any special equipment is necessary, or if they're planning a speaker dinner). What they tell you can give you a sense as to how organized the event will be—ideally, you want to work with a well-oiled machine. I've spoken at events that totally have their act together, as well as events where they couldn't provide water (see my first keynote). A loosely run event doesn't spell disaster, but if you're worried about communication or technical snags, you might want a conference that's more organized.
- **Other speakers' topics:** ask what the other speakers have planned to talk about. I've had a "whoops!" moment where, after signing the contract, the event organizer realized that another speaker and I were talking about *exactly the same* topic, and we had to work backward to see if we could each tweak our talks to make them complement each other rather than overlap. Ensure that you're maximizing the audience's learning and setting yourself up for success.

And remember, just because an event has accepted your proposal, it *doesn't* mean you must say yes. As you move into specifics, you might decide the event doesn't align with your values, what you want to share with the audience, or what you want to get out of giving a talk. Don't hesitate to decline; I promise, it won't have a bearing on whether you're invited to other events in the future.

After you sign

Gather as much information as you can from the organizers. More specific logistics like the technical setup, flow of the day, and what they need from you will shape how you create your talk—so ask away.

Try questions like these:

- "When will I go on? First thing? Last thing? Right after lunch?" (This information will help you figure out how much caffeine to down, how much energy your audience might have, and how you fit into the tone of the day.)
- "Will you record the talk? Will it be made public?"
- "What aspect ratio should I use for my slides?" (Getting this right means you won't have black bars on either side of the screen when your slides are projected.)
- "Can I use my own laptop, or will I need to upload slides to a shared laptop at the event? If shared, what are acceptable file formats?"
- "What kind of adapters do I need to connect my laptop to the projector?"
- "Is it possible to play video or share audio from my laptop while onstage?"
- "I plan on showing a demo and need the internet. Do you have a separate Wi-Fi network or wired connection for speakers?" (Crowded Wi-Fi can be a major problem for demos.)

Put together a conference profile with the answers to these questions. For example, developer Anna Debenham collects notes on each event she's spoken at, including contact info, packing lists, itinerary, etc. She also adds a photo of the inside of the venue, so she has a sense of the space before she arrives. See her template to start your own (https://gist.github.com/maban/d0e4e3336edacf0224db).

Conference profiles are tremendously helpful if you're speaking at more than one event. Plus, you'll have a place to document your experience at the event and what you learned afterward. Better yet, you can share it with other speakers who come and ask *you* for help finding a venue.

Congratulations! You've found your topic and your venue—it's time to start writing!

CHAPTER FOUR

Writing your presentation

Y OUR TOPIC HAS BEGUN TO TAKE SHAPE, you have a venue in mind, maybe you can even picture yourself onstage...it's becoming real now!

When you think about the entire timeline for talk prep from start to finish, I'm guessing the bulk of your process will be spent on the writing stage. This may be obvious, but it's worth saying: give yourself enough time to write the presentation, iterate, and gather feedback before officially giving the talk.

Why?

Almost all of the fears shared in my public speaking survey—fears like saying something wrong, missing the mark on what the audience wants, or fumbling onstage—can be alleviated with a healthy amount of preparation. Building in enough time lets you have the space (mental and temporal) to test and work things out with far less stress.

Your talk narrative and slide design will absolutely evolve, and the more you can dedicate to this part of the process, the faster you'll find what works for you. This means *not* procrastinating (I'm sorry!). But if you devote the energy to starting early, you'll have more time to craft an amazing narrative and ensure your message will resonate with your audience.

Content structure

Coherency—avoiding word barf, being articulate—is a natural concern. Many survey respondents feared "not getting points across" or "being boring or rambling." One person worried about "making the story flow well enough...finding the balance between helping people along and having them learn things on their own."

Creating a solid structure for your content is the best way to guide your audience through your topic—structure helps set expectations for what's next, strengthen your arguments, and keep folks more engaged. It also gives you a foothold if you lose your train of thought.

My friend Ed Davis taught me how to put together a presentation that tells a story. Early in drafting one of my first talks, I'd written what I thought was a decent deck: I'd listed the steps involved in making a website faster, with every point backed by plenty of technical detail—think lots of charts, lots of code samples. Ed had some gentle feedback: though the information was clear, he thought my message would better stick with my audience if I could walk them through the context—what made the work important. He suggested I take the audience on a narrative journey:

- **Landscape:** what exists. In my presentation, the landscape was "A lot of web pages load slowly."
- **Analysis:** what you, the presenter, want to highlight for the audience about that landscape. "This poor performance creates a poor user experience."
- **Problem:** the core issue based on your analysis. "Studies have shown a correlation between a slow site and decreased engagement, which isn't what website owners want."
- **Options:** what we could do. "We could ignore it! Or we could speed up the site in these ways."

- **Solution:** the best option and how it works. This was the bulk of my talk, walking through all the ways to improve front-end performance.
- **Reasons:** why the audience should believe you. "Completing this work sped up the site by 35% and increased conversions by 7%."
- **Bigger idea:** why this concept matters even if it seems irrelevant to an audience member's work. "Even if you think your site is fast, what's the experience for your users on slower infrastructure, outdated mobile networks, or older devices?"

I'll be honest: I didn't think much of this new narrative. I was building a slide deck on techniques to improve page load time. Wouldn't people—people who were *choosing* to see my talk—already know why performance was important? Why should I add the landscape, the bigger idea? Enough fluff—don't people just want the *how*?

Thankfully, I decided to give this narrative structure a shot (uncomfortable feedback is often a gift—we'll talk about that more in Chapter 5). Immediately, the presentation was *so much better*: the story helped draw in the audience, and the logical progression meant they could follow my flow and trust my arguments.

Developing this presentation structure also forced me to ask myself: *Why am I even speaking to begin with?* Nailing down the bigger idea—what I wanted the audience to leave with and think about after they went home—was crucial to making my presentation memorable.

This sample narrative structure won't work for everyone, of course. You have plenty to pick from; a couple include incorporating a backstory or flashback, or following the Hero's Journey (https://en.wikipedia.org/wiki/Hero%27s_journey). Your topic may work best with more case studies, graphs, or live demonstrations.

Whatever tack you take, think about the talks that have resonated the most with you. What kind of narrative or structure did the presenter follow? Why did it work so well? How did they make their arguments stick?

The most important part of your presentation is what happens *after*; use your presentation to lead your audience to both inspiration and concrete next steps.

Crafting slides

Your slides serve two audiences: the crowd and *you*. You want your slides to help the audience best digest the information you're sharing, but you also want to feel comfortable delivering your message.

Everyone has their own method of making a deck—some like to hammer out the exact words they'd like to say, others choose to use slides as a rough outline, adding notes as they go. Whatever your order of operations, I suggest making sure your narrative is ready before worrying too much about how it looks.

Incorporating visuals

Slides act as visual support, set the pace, help you remember where you are in your narrative, and pique your audience's interest.

The first step is figuring out what parts of your talk need visual reinforcement. Let's start with the obvious: intros and titles, key points, transitions, resources, contact info, an end of talk thank you. Do you have info that's best represented visually, like any charts, maps, code examples, before and after screenshots? Pop it on a slide. If you're anxious about rushing through your talk, limit yourself to one major thought per slide for a more consistent rhythm. Choose text and/or imagery that cues up what you want to say.

The next step is focusing on how the audience digests your content—how your slides look is a major element:

- **Color:** some presenters assign meaning to colors, so an audience may subtly follow the narrative; I like to use a different background color for each "chapter" of my talk.
- **Text:** pick "sound bytes"—a line 140 characters or less—to give your audience something tweetable to share and remember as you speak in depth on the idea.
- **Imagery:** Some people forgo text altogether, and exclusively use photographs and other kinds of images to keep visual interest and support their speech, without making the audience read. Which is a fair point: slides can also be a major potential distraction for your audience, because it's really hard to multitask reading and listening (and any note-taking).
- **Clarity:** review your deck to see if you have any extra-long sentences, or visuals that may be tough to parse.

A final note: slide design is very personal. Feel empowered to make choices about the presentation of your information that works best for you, the content, and the event. Don't be afraid to try things out. I've seen half-hour talks that blast through hundreds of slides without the audience noticing, and others with five slides. Or zero slides. Your audience won't be counting. Just ensure however you go about crafting them, your slides benefit both you and the people in the crowd.

Accessibility and inclusivity

While you'll put your own spin on slide design, comprehension is still paramount. Triple-check your content is easy to see and scan—your audience shouldn't have to spend more energy parsing tiny, low-contrast text than listening to your message.

Pay attention to typefaces and colors—too many of either can distract your audience. Use color accessibility tools, like Lea Verou's Contrast Ratio (http://leaverou.github.io/contrast-ratio/), to verify your content is readable by people with color blindness or other visual impairments. Taking steps to improve readability will help everybody in an audience: test your slides from a distance to mimic sitting in the back row, staring at a projector. Can you read the text without issue?

Another element to consider is whether your event will have an interpreter, spoken or signed. In her post "Interpretation," Anna Debenham noted ways to make their jobs easier (http://www.maban.co.uk/97):

- Complete your slides well in advance so the interpreter can prepare
- Discuss with the interpreter beforehand any content they can skip
- Remove any cultural references a non-domestic audience might not understand, or choose more global examples

Last but definitely not least, turn your critical eye to inclusivity. As the person onstage, you wield some influence—you can actively counter stereotypes, biases, and assumptions your audience (and you!) may have.

In a Technically Speaking webinar, Judith Williams shares a terrific checklist to vet your images (https://www.youtube.com/watch?v=cS3a4t2C3AA):

- Are you showing people who are different from you?
- Are you showing a variety of people doing different things?
- Are you actively trying to challenge our stereotypes and biases?

This helps root out unconscious biases too. I've seen presentations filled with reaction GIFs of exclusively white people, or stock images of men in management and technical roles and women in customer service.

Apply the Williams test to the rest of your slide content: your case study examples, stories, user personas, etc. Please, please don't conflate "moms" with "technology rubes"—avoid lines like, "So easy even a mom could understand!" Switch between "he" and "she" when you share hypothetical examples about people; better yet, stick with "they," which works for both individuals and groups. Noninclusive rhetoric and imagery can be incredibly distracting, if not harmful.

Your job as a speaker is to make your slides and message accessible to your entire audience; take the extra time and care to ensure you're using your influence well.

Bells and whistles

So you want to get a little impressive with your presentation, maybe take it to the next level? These next elements are definitely optional—use them at your own discretion, if at all. Remember, it's up to you.

Technical extras

If it suits your content and style, you can add audio, transitions and animations, and live demos. In the public speaking survey, people wrote they feared having their demos fail or "making stupid coding mistakes" during their talk. There are some elements to technology that are out of your control, and getting fancier with your presentation may leave you more susceptible. Luckily, you have time to create backup plans should things go haywire (in Chapter 6, we'll run through a technical checklist once you're at the venue).

Aside from internet access, projector connections, etc., one big piece of prep is to sort out the timing of your slides. Some slide software slows down when you include animations or transitions, creating a delay when you click to advance. I've witnessed similar slowdowns when someone projects slides over a webcast or other video. Be sure to practice syncing your talk to your slides, and account for potential lags. If you're aiming to work through a lot of slides fast, you might skip animations in your deck.

Mid-conference and post-talk resources

None of us do our work in a vacuum—it's good web citizenship to promote others' work, and to help your audience continue to learn after your presentation.

If you do a little homework before the conference, you can uncover which speakers have topics related to yours. Reference their names and talk times in a slide or two, and recommend that people check them out.

With even *more* preparation, you might contact those speakers early on how you can dovetail your narratives. For instance, when designer Yesenia Perez-Cruz and I were both speaking at the same event, we worked together to ensure we didn't overlap in our content: she chose to focus on performance from a designer's perspective, sharing real-life examples of weighing aesthetics and site speed, while I followed her talk with a deep dive into tactics for optimizing a site once the initial designs are done. By working together (however loosely), you can build on each other's content or net your audience different spins on the same topic.

You might also amass a list of resources for audience members to browse post-talk. Share the list in a slide, and reference the link throughout your talk. I like to have a link to every tool, study, and article I cited or used as inspiration. I organize the links in chronological order (if I only have a few), or group them into subheadings like "Case Studies" and "Tools" (if I have a bunch). For extra credit, add links to helpful content that didn't quite fit into your talk but is a terrific springboard if people want to explore deeper.

For each link, use bit.ly or another click-tracking service. This tidies your URLs, but better yet, you'll be able to see which resources get more traffic after your talk. What is your audience interested in? This is one way to gather data that will help you measure your success and iterate on your presentation.

One last tip: at the top of the resources slide, I'll host a copy of the slides, so everything is in one place. I like sharing the online version of my talk to hopefully reach and help a wider audience. Some conferences, and some presenters, aren't comfortable having this information freely available. Do what works for you, your audience, and the event.

Presenter notes

Just as your slides are an aid to your audience, your presenter notes are an aid to you. Use this private content to make you feel as comfortable as possible onstage. Your notes can take on a variety of styles; choose one that works for you. Some speakers include full sentences, and others stick with short phrases to jog their memory. Some use the presenter notes built into their slide software, and others write them down or read from a tablet.

Are you worried about forgetting your words? Include clues. If you're just starting to practice your talk, there's no harm in including everything you want to say or do. I've gone so far as to type reminders to click to advance the slide or trigger an animation. You can always trim your notes as you get more familiar with your presentation, and rely on them less and less. Worried about speaking too fast? Remind yourself to breathe! Give yourself lots of big pauses to help your future self take it easy on the stage.

Whatever your approach, make sure your notes are accessible and easy to read, like your slides. Preview how they look: check that the font is large enough, use short and easy-to-scan phrases or bullets, and don't write so much you'll have to scroll through them while onstage. Lean on them as little or as much as you'd like—and adapt them accordingly. Your notes are there to help appease your public speaking fears.

Holding the audience's attention

The goal of your presentation is to convey information—to make sure what you're sharing *lands*, without distracting your audience. You have many opportunities to engage your audience and hold their attention—let's look at a few ways to do so.

Incorporate humor

Humor can be a great tool—get people laughing, and they'll probably be engaged with what you have to say. The right level of levity and timing can serve as a deep breath after a big drop of information, put people at ease, and help hold attention through to the end.

But humor can also be tough to incorporate and deliver; survey respondents definitely worried their jokes would fall flat. My personal presentation style is fairly poised; I sneak in a few subtle jokes, but delivering content like a stand-up comedian wouldn't feel natural to me. Other speakers take on a rough-around-the-edges, funny persona, and the energy works with their style. Do what makes you feel the most comfortable and confident in sharing information with your audience.

If you choose to use humor, practice and run it by a few people to make sure the jokes (and GIFs!) land. If you include memes, triple-check where they originated and see if they carry additional meanings. I've seen well-meaning presenters incorporate memes with racist or sexist histories, and the presenters didn't seem to have a clue about their context. Tread carefully; your best bet is to do your research and get feedback from a wide range of other perspectives.

Set audience expectations

My coworker Bill Massie is a phenomenal public speaker; he always keeps the audience enraptured and receives raucous applause. Fascinatingly, Bill breaks one of the major "rules" of public speaking every time he gives a talk: he reads from his notes. The key is when Bill speaks, he acknowledges his note-reading to the audience at the start. What might be a distraction works in his favor: he lets us know *he* knows he's going against the "norm," and we stop thinking about it.

Set expectations for your audience upfront, so they have their ears and brains open to your content. Some presenters share an agenda or intro slide that gives a quick overview of what they'll cover. Some talk descriptions include a list of takeaways, so the audience knows what they're in for and why they should attend. When possible, within the first few minutes of being onstage, I like to frame my talk as it relates to other speakers at the conference, explaining how my work contrasts with or builds on their topics. Keep your audience in mind as you craft your slides: What early expectations should you set for them?

Keep 'em on their toes

Asking the audience questions helps inject jolts of energy. I open a lot of talks by asking people to raise their hands as I call out job titles, so I get a sense of how many identify as developers, designers, etc. I'll find other sneaky ways of checking in throughout the presentation: "Does anybody spot the outlier on this graph?" During one talk, I asked the audience to tweet at me once they'd implemented the performance techniques I'd covered, promising to send a T-shirt to the person who sped up their site the most. Little interactions sprinkled throughout a talk helps significantly with keeping folks' attention.

Time it

Time your delivery and make sure your content fits your talk slot. Whether you like to keep a quick pace or expound on each and every slide, getting the timing down absolutely takes work. It's also your job: as a speaker at an event, you affect how the day is running. If you go over your allotted time, you're pushing into the schedules of other speakers. (Or you might be the affected speaker—and organizers might ask you to help get the schedule back on track by going under.)

Do the work to ensure you'll get your message across within your time onstage. Run through your slide deck. As you practice, note where you have flexibility: Which aspects could you spend more time on, or cut if necessary? You have control over how you divvy up your overall slot. The amount of time for Q&A, if you choose to do one, is almost always up to you; some speakers really enjoy answering a large number of audience questions after they're done speaking, and others prefer a handful, or none at all. (We'll talk more on ways to hold a Q&A session in Chapter 7.)

In my experience, going under time is fine. Sometimes I'll answer more questions, or riff further on a closing idea. Or I'll end the session a bit early, as people appreciate the extra buffer to take restroom breaks or network in the hallway track. Begin to learn your content well enough so that you can reference relevant sections during Q&A, and know which parts you can linger on or speed up if needed.

Iterate on it

You've gone through a few practice rounds and are settling into your draft. It's *almost* time to share your talk with others, but first take the opportunity to reflect and edit on your own. Revising a little now will help you determine what you truly want to say—so you can be more clear about your goals when you ask for feedback.

Here are some questions to ready your work for others:
- Is the talk compelling enough? Will it inspire your audience?
- Check the event's description of your talk. Does it match what you've created?
- Do you see any potential distraction points for the audience you should remove or rephrase?
- Do you have unnecessary or filler content? Or is anything missing?
- How will people with different levels of experience react to your talk? Should you give more context and explanation? Less?

Picture your future audience as you revise. When you were writing the talk, you might've pictured yourself or someone you know well listening and learning from your words. Now put yourself in your future audience's shoes; they're probably strangers to you, and it's your job to do right by them. Will they enjoy your sense of humor? Will they understand why you think this topic is so important? Will they learn something new?

You may find yourself with some writer's block at this stage. That's okay! It can be hard to keep a level head as you time and iterate your talk ad infinitum—you get too close to the words and ideas. If you can, take some time away. Or do what I do when I get stuck: bring in others for a fresh perspective. Let's clear the page, and talk about talking in front of other people.

CHAPTER FIVE

Practicing and gathering feedback

THE ACT OF GETTING ONSTAGE and speaking on a topic introduces a tremendous amount of vulnerability. Day to day, we navigate mistakes and correct them in front of a very small audience—we rarely spend so much time preparing work with only *one shot* to nail the delivery of that work.

A large percentage of survey respondents shared fears about being or appearing inarticulate; one worried about "talking too fast and sounding unprepared (even when I'm super prepared)." And many people were concerned about being wrong:

- "Discovering mid-talk I know less about the topic than everyone in the audience does."
- "Being judged, saying something wrong and going viral."
- "Phrasing something incorrectly and having the internet blow up about it."

You can set yourself up for success and comfort onstage with repeated practice ahead of time. Practicing by yourself or with a trusted group of listeners will enable you to get feedback and test out approaches to Q&A.

Rehearsing your talk is an extremely personal endeavor. For you, practicing might mean sitting at your desk, saying your words in your head as you advance your slides. Perhaps it means standing up in an empty conference room, to get a sense of how far away your laptop will be and what a remote feels like in your hands. Or recording a test run for yourself to review later. Or gathering your friends to watch, so you can practice keeping eye contact and reading the room.

My best advice is to focus on one aspect at a time. When you think about giving your talk, which parts feel most unfamiliar? How confident do you feel about using a microphone or what to do with your hands? What's the balance between reading from your notes and looking at the audience? Adopt a method that prioritizes the areas you want to get comfortable with first.

How much should you practice? It *absolutely* depends on you. I like to go through my talks half a dozen times alone before asking coworkers to listen and weigh in. I find my flow and start to get comfortable with my word choices throughout the narrative before sharing it with more people. But try not to overdo it—too much prep can make you grow tired of your words or topic. It's okay to take a breather after lots of practicing; for example, I won't practice the day before an event, so 1) the talk feels fresh, and 2) I don't think I've already said something onstage when I really said it in a dry run yesterday. With time—and yep, practice—you'll figure out the right rehearsal flow for you.

Practicing solo

Let's start with a warm-up: run through your talk by yourself. Take a moment to list what you want to get from it:

- Do you want to simply go through the entire talk without stopping?
- Do you want to get used to the sound of your voice?

- Do you want to check the timing of your slides or the overall flow?
- Do you want to nail down your wording?
- Do you want to focus on more technical aspects, like getting comfortable using your computer in presentation mode?

Articulating a goal for each run-through gives you a concrete way to mark your progress, and hopefully breaks the practicing process into digestible, achievable parts.

Note that standing up for rehearsals can feel very different from staying seated—your pace, body language, and gestures may change. You'll want to adapt to the distance between you and your computer (or presenter notes), and you might adjust how you hold the remote or use the keyboard. If you're worried about the strangeness of being onstage, you might recreate your talk's conditions: rig a podium and practice while standing.

One last bit: keep going—don't stop and restart every time you get tripped up. Designer Dave Shea suggests, "Learn how to talk your way out of a factual error [...], speaking flub, or even just simple mispronunciation" (http://mezzoblue.com/archives/2006/02/27/speaking_ti/). If you're able to work through a mistake in a practice run, you'll have confidence you can do so again should it happen onstage.

Practicing with people

You've gotten the hang of your talk as a whole; now level-up your game by practicing in front of a (small) crowd. You'll get fresh minds and ears and can vet specific sections, and see if folks are left with any lingering questions. Even better, this is your chance to gather nonverbal feedback and practice reading the room. As you relax into your talk, watch how people respond: do they laugh? Do they lean toward you and look focused? Are they nodding? Or do they look confused or distracted? By tracking this kind of feedback, you'll develop a sense about which parts of your presentation are more engaging, move too quickly, or should be further workshopped.

So who should be in your practice group (or as I like to call them, the "feedback crew")? Draw from your coworkers, friends, and other peers. (I like to limit it to three to four people, at least at first.) It's helpful if they have attended or spoken at conferences. Try to have a range of job titles or levels of experience, as more backgrounds will give you a better perspective on how accessible or interesting your talk is to a wider audience. You could also organize different groups (all speakers, all junior developers, mixed crowd, etc.) for different types of feedback (like asking speakers particular questions about your slide design).

If practicing in front of people is less than comfortable, but you'd like feedback on narrative, word choice, or other non-body-language aspects of the presentation, consider recording a dry run privately. My coworker Ian Malpass practices alone, records his talk on his computer, and then sends it to others to get their thoughts asynchronously (http://www.indecorous.com/writing_talks/). This lets him dedicate time and focus to each separate activity (practicing, receiving feedback), and gives him the mental space to shift gears.

Equip your crew to give good feedback

It can be nerve-wracking to request feedback, let alone on something as personal and anxiety-inducing as public speaking. But on the bright side, you probably already make use of these same skills—giving and receiving feedback—at your job: helming design critiques or code reviews, presenting to your team or to clients, designing and developing…*anything*. In any of these settings, it's key to set expectations for your feedback-givers and prepare yourself to absorb their notes.

Do the same for your feedback crew. Give them details about your presentation, the audience, and what kind of feedback you're looking for. Here are some questions to answer for them before you start:

- How long is your speaking slot? How much talking time (versus Q&A) are you aiming for?

- What's the audience like? Do they specialize in a certain area? What's their technical depth?
- When is your talk? Early or late? Right before or after lunch?

Guide your crew through your practice run too—ask for general impressions, but prompt them with specific questions you'd like them to think on as they listen. Depending on the feedback you're after (which may change depending on where you are in the editing process), pick a few from these lists:

Topic and technical depth

- Is the message easy to understand? Are there any confusing sections or missing points?
- Are any terms unfamiliar or need more context?
- How does the content line up with your expectations? Does it match the talk description?
- What do you think the audience will ask in the Q&A?
- Does this inspire the audience to try something new? Or do more research afterward?

Slide design

- Can you read everything on the slides? Will people in the back of a large room be able to?
- Does each slide offer the right amount of info? Are you spending more time reading than listening?
- Do any of the slides have extraneous content? (Browser window add-ons, dates from email screenshots, irrelevant code in snippets, etc.)
- Are fonts, colors, and other design elements consistent?

Narrative

- Do you feel yourself tuning out at any point? Are there any spots where I get too into the weeds?
- What parts are most compelling to you?

- Did any words, slang, references, or jokes catch you by surprise or otherwise distract you?
- How effective is the bigger idea at the end? Is the takeaway meaningful even if someone already knows the meat of the talk?

Presentation style

This can be a sensitive topic! Feel free to have your feedback crew send pointers in private.

- Do I do anything distracting with my hands, body, or voice?
- How engaged with the audience do I seem? How much do I rely on presentation notes? Do I look locked to my laptop?
- How does the tone suit the topic? (For example, is humor helpful or distracting?)
- Do I say anything (or have any imagery) that could be interpreted as racist, sexist, ableist, etc.?

Next-level feedback

Get the know-how from those who have been there: here are some questions to ask experienced presenters or topic experts.

- Would any of the visualizations benefit from an animation, a screen capture, or other slide design technique?
- What feedback do you have on my resources page? Are there other people or links I should add?
- If you've presented at this conference or in this country before, can you share any tips from your experience?
- Are there any constraints from the conference organizers I should try to push back on for the sake of the audience? (Required slide design, room setup, etc.)

Equip yourself to receive feedback

After the run-through, thank your audience and take a moment to shift your brain into feedback-receiving mode. Let your crew know *how* you'd like to receive their thoughts and *when*. Maybe you're energized from your practice talk, and want to high-five and dive right into a conversation then and there. Or maybe you're a little drained, and you aren't ready for feedback just yet. It's okay to request comments separately and in a different medium! You can ask people to email you, or talk about it over coffee later. You could even create an anonymous form for folks to fill out. Whatever makes you feel comfortable (and thus more receptive). Remember, we're working on reducing fear, and your feedback crew will want to help and support you.

If you're especially worried about receiving hard-to-hear feedback, consider setting up two more bumper guards: a card-suit rubric, and a questions-first approach.

LifeLabs Learning (http://lifelabsnewyork.com/) developed a rubric, which uses suits to describe four different kinds of feedback:

- **Hearts:** feedback that is positive, but not specific. "I really liked your talk!"
- **Diamonds:** feedback that is positive, and specific or actionable. "I thought your talk was funny, especially that joke about frogs. It held my attention."
- **Clubs:** feedback that is negative, but not specific or constructive. "I thought your talk was boring."
- **Spades:** feedback that is negative, but gives specific suggestions. "My mind started to wander when you described the technical changes. Could you include more screenshots or other visuals to help keep the audience's attention?"

It's a great shorthand for getting the feedback you'd like—explain these to your crew, and ask for diamonds and spades.

Second, ask your feedback crew to open with questions before jumping into specific observations. For instance, when I'm part of a practice audience, I like to ask, "How did you feel about that?" as a presenter finishes their dry run. Then I work to listen and understand what they're thinking and feeling before I offer suggestions. It's a friendlier framing to ask someone, "How comfortable did you feel onstage?" rather than, "You seemed locked to your laptop." It gives them a chance to reflect, and maybe even realize it on their own—a win-win for everyone.

Distill the feedback

Part of what makes diamond and spade feedback so valuable is the focus on an actionable item—it gives you something specific to respond to. If your feedback crew is sharing more hearts or clubs, ask open questions to turn their feedback toward the concrete. For example: "Can you help me understand why I should include a code sample?" or "What specifically about that story felt dull? Do you think it's the wording or the imagery—or something else?"

This may be strange to hear now, but: not all feedback is valuable, and not all feedback needs to be incorporated. Hopefully you've cultivated a feedback crew you can count on to provide thoughtful, honest critique. But responses are also subjective; everyone has their own opinions and style. You know best what you want to say—and whether you'll feel comfortable delivering it onstage.

Some folks' suggestions may rely on presentation "rules" or their personal style. What feels comfortable to them might not to you (which is normal). Step back, and see if their feedback makes your points clearer or reduces audience distraction. If it doesn't, feel free to discard.

Sometimes, you might receive feedback that's upsetting or catches you off guard—again, it's okay to put some time and distance between receiving and responding to others' thoughts. Talk it over with a trusted friend, or someone else in the feedback crew. When you feel up to it, follow up on that feedback with clarifying questions ("Can you give me an example of how to incorporate that note?" or "How do you think the audience will respond differently to that change") to help you understand how the feedback is intended and how you want to take it into account.

Over time, you'll get better at sorting through everyone's comments. And in my experience, asking more questions and workshopping ways to address feedback has given me a more diverse perspective on how people receive my content and tone.

One last thing to consider: it *is* up to you, but stay open to being pushed out of your comfort zone. People want to be helpful, and you've chosen a smart crew, so it's worth paying special attention if the feedback feels tough to digest. When you get constructive criticism, recognize that that person thinks it's important enough to share despite the discomfort in delivering it. There will be times when you need to let go of jokes or when your favorite bit isn't doing enough work for you. Your feedback crew represents your future audience. This is the time to prioritize your future audience's needs over your own.

Practicing Q&A

When in doubt, practice, and this holds for answering audience questions as well. For me, those questions are my favorite part of a talk—I love the opportunity to interact with folks, learn about the problems they're dealing with, and try to help them.

But I understand why tons of survey respondents worried about how Q&A *might* go. It seems we've either witnessed or imagined lots of extreme audience participation. People feared:

- "Not understanding the questions."
- "Someone pointing out a hole in my premise that I entirely overlooked—being judged and found incompetent."
- "Being belittled because someone in the audience knows (or thinks they know) more about my topic than I do."
- "Being called out by someone who knows more."

We all want to do well. We want to write a good talk and deliver it in a way that keeps people engaged and learning. We want it to land! The fears expressed here have less to do with how much time and effort you put into crafting a solid presentation with clear examples and takeaways; that amount of work is fully in your control. What's *less* in your control is how the audience responds to it, or what they might think of it and you.

Let's break down those fears. What I'm hearing underneath those statements are three primary concerns:

- Not knowing the answer to a question (or how to handle not knowing)
- Being revealed as an impostor
- Facing aggression from an audience member

Running a practice Q&A can help you vet answers and phrasing, get comfortable saying "I don't know," and develop strategies and coping mechanisms for those key fears. Ask your feedback crew for some follow-up questions about your topic. Once you feel good on that front, you can level up your prep and ask to field tougher questions.

Ask your test audience to imagine creative ways people could misunderstand your point, go on complete tangents, give incorrect information, or bring up typical arguments that go nowhere (like, "But isn't X a better language than Y?"). Maybe they say something silly or weirdly aggressive. (We'll talk more about how to handle aggression and harassment in Chapter 7.)

My major breakthrough in public speaking was when I realized I could say, "I don't know." No matter how deep of an expert you are on a topic, there will *always* be questions you're unprepared to answer. I've said "I don't know" to:

- Questions I probably knew the answer to, but couldn't hear or didn't understand the phrasing.
- Questions that were totally off-base and missed the point of the presentation.
- Questions I plain didn't know the answer to.

It is *absolutely fine* to say "I don't know" when you're onstage. You're being honest, and the audience (the vast majority) will be in your corner. After all, they probably just learned a ton from you! "I don't know" isn't a disappointment or proof you shouldn't be onstage. You have many ways to say it in a positive and encouraging way:

- "Oh, I don't know the answer to that question. I'll look it up after this session is done and tweet what I find, though!"
- "Oh, hmm, I actually don't know. Could anyone else in the audience help us out?"
- "Oh, that's interesting, I haven't thought about that before. I'd be happy to chat more with you afterward!"

Say "I don't know" and continue forward with a smile to the next question—the more you practice this, the more comfortable you'll be. But even if you're sweating in the moment, remember this very important piece of information: *the audience is rooting for you.*

Yes, exceptions may exist—but have you ever attended a talk and actively rooted *against* a speaker? Have you watched a speaker get tongue-tied, asked a rough question, or lose their train of thought? Probably, and you probably cheered for them to make a comeback, regain their composure, and charge on to deliver the rest of their talk. Extend that kindness to yourself and your presentation. Know it's okay if you slip up, and know your audience will understand.

(We are all rooting for you.)

CHAPTER SIX

Counting down

Let's pause and reflect on the loads of work you've done. You've chosen and workshopped a topic you really want to share with the world. You've found the right venue, learned about its audience, and went and drafted a great talk. You practiced and iterated your presentation—pushing places that'll resonate with your audience and give them something to chew on afterward. Your talk is well on its way to being an enormous success.

Now that we're counting down to the days leading up to the event, let yourself lean back a little, and take a big breath. Shift your thinking to preparing and packing, following up on event logistics, and easing any anxiety that may pop up now. Most of all, congratulate yourself on nearing the home stretch.

Prepare and pack

From clothing to adapters, from backups to business cards, let's tackle your suitcase or conference go bag. What's here won't work for everybody or every event, but I hope to provide an overview of options for you to consider—so you can feel settled in knowing you've set yourself up for action and comfort.

Wear what makes you feel like a superhero

I've spent a lot of time thinking on my appearance as a speaker. How much of "me" do I want to be onstage? Should I present a more polished, "public speaker" self? What's okay to wear, and how does that affect my delivery or the way the audience perceives me?

These are tricky questions. Part of the worry, echoed by survey participants, is about "authenticity"—the idea that a good speaker should show their *truest* self to be relatable and engaging.

But, as engineering professor Deb Chachra writes, "performance, by definition, isn't 'authentic'" (https://tinyletter. com/metafoundry/letters/metafoundry-48-embarrassingly- parallel-problems). The person you are onstage will not—and doesn't need to be—the most "authentic" version of you, because, frankly, being onstage isn't your normal habitat. As Chachra points out, "I doubt that Bjork or Amanda Palmer or Lady Gaga or David Bowie feel inauthentic for having on-stage personae." Putting on a persona or character can give you some healthy emotional distance and make you feel more powerful— and it's okay to take advantage of that. For me, my outfit comes down to wearing whatever makes me feel confident—and letting that "whatever" change over time, and mean different things in different venues. While I do get significantly more (unhelpful) feedback about my tone when I wear a dress and heels to present than when I wear a T-shirt and jeans, I still choose to dress a little nicer than I do day to day. That extra effort is a way for me to show I take the event and work seriously, and it gets me in the mindset to deliver an awesome talk.

Think about what clothing would get you in that mindset for your own talk—what would make you feel like a superhero? What could you wear that will help you feel the strongest, most secure, and grounded while onstage?

Hold that superhero uniform in your brain, and then see if it holds up against an onstage scenario. Here are some factors to consider as you pick your public-speaking outfit:

Avoiding wardrobe malfunctions

- Pick lightweight, airy clothes that won't stick to your skin (stage lights can be really warm).
- Darker clothes can help hide sweat stains. Consider packing a small handkerchief, if you want to wipe your forehead during the talk.
- Keep microphone placement in mind. Avoid scarves and jewelry (necklaces, pins) that might bump into the mic.
- Test your outfit for movement, especially if you tend to roam the stage or make wide gestures.
- Check your button-down shirt for gaps (befriend double-sided tape).

Working with the stage setup

- Try to see what the stage will look like: find pictures of the venue online or ask the organizers. If the curtain backdrop skews dark, you might avoid wearing all-black, so you aren't camouflaged.
- If the event plans on taping talks, consider what works well onscreen. Stripes and other patterns can create banding on recordings, so you might opt for solids.
- If you wear makeup, you may want to apply it more heavily because the bright lights could wash it out.
- Test your clothes under fluorescent (or other ultra-bright) lighting for any stains or sheerness that may be less visible in your home lighting.

I always recommend packing backups of, well, everything. If you're able, pack an alternative outfit. You never know what might happen on the day of an event, and it's far less stressful to have options. If you wear heels, consider bringing flats just in case.

Pack an electronics bag

It isn't only you onstage—it's your electronics too! Think through the equipment you'll need to ensure you won't have to scramble to get everything connected correctly moments before you go on.

- If you use a remote to advance your slides, I recommend choosing a very simple one with few buttons—the more buttons, the more chances you might accidentally tap one that does something unexpected to your presentation. Also: pack backup batteries.
- If you're using your own laptop, don't forget to ask what kinds of adapters you'll need to connect your computer to the projector. I take along both VGA and DVI adapters.
- Remember your power adapters (especially if you need a MagSafe one). If you're traveling abroad, pack an international power adapter kit.
- Consider an ethernet cable, for speedier internet (particularly if you're running demos). I also bring an ethernet adapter, as my MacBook Air doesn't have an ethernet port.
- Consider a USB hub to charge all your devices at once, instead of hunting down individual wall outlets.

Placing these electronics accessories into a dedicated bag will make it easier for you to retrieve an item later. Plus, you can keep one electronics bag packed at all times and continue to use it at each speaking event without worrying about forgetting something.

Back up everything

No matter how confident you are that you'll be able to use your own equipment onstage, prepare for that *just in case* moment when you'll need to use someone else's machine. Their laptop might have different software or fonts installed, and the last thing you want to do is rush to reformat everything so it works correctly onstage.

To avoid this pitfall (and major spike in stress), I suggest two safeties. One, create a backup folder of your files and save it to a physical thumb drive. Two, save the folder online in whatever service you prefer (I use Dropbox) and email the link to yourself. This way, you can quickly forward that link to someone else, if they need your files. Your backups should include:

- Your original slide deck (PowerPoint file, Keynote file, HTML, etc.)
- Any fonts used in your presentation
- A PDF of your slide deck without notes, so if another person's laptop can't run your original deck, you can still show your PDF as slides (though animated GIFs and videos won't work)
- A PDF of your slide deck *with* notes, so you can reference them from a tablet or phone if necessary

Triple-check your logistics

When you're presenting a live demonstration of a technique, workflow, or product, be prepared for things to go wrong. If you're supplying a service, open-sourcing some code, or promoting a product, check that it's accessible to your audience—capacity-plan to ensure it can handle the oncoming traffic.

If your presentation needs the internet, include a low-tech alternative on a thumb drive. For example, save a PDF to display the code you wanted to demonstrate, or save a video of your planned live demo. When possible, you could also record a simple screen capture of your demo to use as a further backup.

If you want to be *exceptionally* prepared, create a second version of your slide deck in the other major aspect ratio. If the conference requested 4:3, create a duplicate in 16:9, and vice versa. This way, should the conference tell you the wrong ratio (which has happened to me!), you're ready with a smart-looking deck anyway.

Revisit what the conference has listed for your talk. Is it still the right date and time? How about the description? Once, after checking what I'd originally written as an abstract for my talk, I realized I'd forgotten to cover one of my intended points!

I edited my talk and deck to sneak in an extra few thoughts on what the audience would expect to see, along with additional links to my resources page so people could read more on the topic later.

Last but not least: pack some business cards!

Travel

Maybe travel is incredibly refreshing for you—kudos!—or maybe it's a ticket to hives. If you're in the second camp, don't worry. With some planning, you can reduce your travel stress and cruise your way to the main event.

Manage energy drain

Travel can drain our energy quickly, no matter how long or short the trip. If you tend to suffer from jet lag, consider arriving earlier than necessary for the event to rest up and feel more like yourself before the big day. If I'm flying internationally, I land a few days early to adjust to the time zone, so I can do my best work when presenting.

Give yourself the space to recharge in the days before your talk. It can be exhausting to travel *and* meet new people, on top of prepping for the spotlight. It's okay to skip networking events, or duck out early from a speaker's dinner or happy hour. Carve out alone time if you need it, and save your energy for the work you'll be doing onstage.

Recognize what's in your control (and what isn't)

Maybe you're concerned about things going *physically* wrong during travel or the event. In the survey, people worried about "feeling sick and having a bad cold," "being unable to speak due to jet lag or lack of sleep and nerves," or "being late to the event." Some of these are in your control, and others are not.

As someone with a chronic illness that affects my mobility and limits my diet, I know I need to sort out a few things on arrival (like where the elevators or escalators are, where to grab food) to give me a sense of control and ease. It's a big help to talk to event organizers about any questions I have on these logistics.

In her article "Make Yourself Comfortable," user researcher Angela Colter writes, "Whatever the requirement may be—a vegetarian food option, allergy-free bedding, or a refrigerator for your medications—acknowledge what it is, then make the request...Just give yourself permission to ask; you don't have to figure it all out on your own" (http://ladiesintech.com/make-yourself-comfortable/). Lean on those around you, and consider what you need to make your experience as comfortable, healthy, and stress-free as possible.

One more way to prepare for the uncertainties in travel: print it out. Pull out your venue profile from Chapter 3, and pack a physical copy. You never know what might happen if you drop your phone or run out of battery when you land in a new place. It can be handy to have information about where you're staying and how to get there (numbers for taxi services, directions for public transportation), and the address of the event itself.

To do at the venue

Shake off the travel dust, and let's explore a few ways to ground yourself and reduce unknowns in your new space. Again, these may not apply to every event, or feel necessary for every speaker, but take what makes sense to you.

A good way to settle in is to confirm the timeline of events leading to your talk:

- Is there a speaker dinner? If so, where and when?
- How much time will you have to prepare the day of your talk?
- When should you eat before and after your talk? Should you set a bedtime the night before to ensure you're well rested?
- How much time will you have to prepare onstage, before your talk starts?

- If you'd like to get an extra rehearsal in, where and when could that happen?
- If you need quiet time to get grounded, where and when can you get some?

If you plan to share your slides online, go ahead and upload your likely final slides to a site like SpeakerDeck or SlideShare; this way, you can share them immediately after your talk. Triple-check your resources page too—make sure the links work and that everything is ready for the public.

Meet and greet

Put faces to names and meet the event organizers and other speakers. These people are now effectively your coworkers—get to know them, ask them for what you need, and be kind and helpful in turn. You're on the same team; you're all there to make the event a success.

You might start by seeking out the speakers' lounge, if the event has one. Unlike the hallway track, it's a low-key, quieter place to chat with people one-on-one or in small groups (and great for decompressing before and after being onstage). If you have any logistical questions, another speaker in the same boat might already have the answer.

Next up, befriend the event staff; I've had plenty of last-minute questions ("Oh, hey, where can I get some water?") and a familiar face can be reassuring. I've asked the person clipping in my microphone if I have food in my teeth, and I've asked the video person to check me for lint. Getting onstage, as we know, is such a vulnerable act—connecting with the people who want to help you do your best work can also help you feel like you have a solid network of support.

Last, check in with the organizers on how you'll be introduced before your talk. See if they have the correct pronunciation of your name, or let them know if you have a preference as to what titles or professional affiliations they include. Some events have an emcee or host (or the organizers themselves) who will introduce you, while some events have no planned introduction—which means you'll be the person stepping onstage to call the audience's attention to your talk. In that case, try a short greeting before clicking through your slide deck: "Good morning! My name is Lara Hogan. I do engineering at Etsy, and I'm here to talk to you about web performance."

Sneak a peek

Whenever possible, scout out where you'll be speaking. Get yourself acquainted with the space and setup (no need to run through your talk—you've already done the prep!). Go onstage: see how it feels under the lights, and how high you are off the ground. You'll sense how far away the audience is, and how close you are to your presenter notes. Look around you: Is anything obstructing your view or the audience's? How does the placement of the table, chair, podium, etc., feel? Definitely consider approaching the organizers if anything seems uncomfortable or distracting. You might be able to shift things around yourself too—but clear it with the organizers to make sure you don't jumble the setup for other speakers.

As you're in the room, you might note A/V technicians or others setting up. Some conferences have very high-tech logistics like custom lighting or music between speakers, while others are more scrappy and it's on the speakers to manage their own equipment. Depending on the event, the staff may help you put on a microphone or test your computer with the A/V system to make sure it works on the day of your talk.

If you can, take advantage of the opportunity to introduce yourself to A/V and ask about the setup. Is there a place to plug in your laptop onstage? Where will you get mic'ed up? What kind of mic will they use? Can you see it or try it on? The more you can get a feel for the onstage logistics, the more at ease you'll be.

Prepare to get onstage

We're in the home stretch! Let's prime you for success on the day of your talk.

Eating and drinking

Along with the mental highs (and worries), public speaking—projecting your voice, gesturing, moving your body, standing in place—is a physical activity. Be sure to fuel yourself.

What you eat and drink depends on your preferences and dietary needs, of course. For me, I also factor in *when* I'm speaking. For example, if I'm presenting first thing in the morning, I might skip breakfast until after the talk, to avoid worrying whether I'll have something in my teeth or whether I'll have enough time to eat a snack before I go onstage. No breakfast means I'll feel way more jittery after a cup of coffee, so I hold out on the caffeine until I'm done.

Onstage, a glass or bottle of water is a convenient prop. For one, it serves as a helpful reminder to slow down during your presentation if you take intermittent sips. For another, it gives you an object to hold, if you feel awkward with your hands. And yes, it hydrates—good if you start coughing or feel your mouth getting dry.

How do I look and sound?

Now's the time to check your pants zipper and any gaps in your button-down shirt. Check for food or lipstick in your teeth, give your appearance a thumbs-up, and head over to get mic'd.

Microphones may throw you for a loop if you're not used to them. Types vary, from what I call "Britney Spears" or head-worn ones that clip to your ear and follow your jawline, to lavalier mics that clip to your collar, to handheld or podium mics. Some microphones require a battery pack, which can be heavy and weigh down your clothing. They generally clip onto your back pocket or belt if you have one; when I wear a dress, I clip the battery pack to the back of my bra.

As you can imagine, getting mic'd up can feel a little awkward, as the audio technician will be close to you and touching your clothes. You can absolutely choose to clip the microphone to yourself in private; don't feel obligated to have the audio technician do it. You can get feedback from them on how you sound through the speakers once you're ready.

Which is another reason to get to know the A/V crew; I've learned a ton from audio teammates as I prepared for the stage. At one conference, I learned head-worn mics aren't fitted for women's faces, often leaving the wire with a lot of extra slack and a poor audio experience. These mics sometimes don't work well for people who wear glasses, or people with long hair that may brush against the microphone. (I, unfortunately, have both.) It was great to be able to talk to the audio person in advance, so we could choose a microphone that would best fit my jawline, glasses, and hairstyle.

But by far my favorite lesson from an audio technician happened when I was wearing a dress made from a thinner fabric that couldn't withstand the weight of a lavalier mic. I apologized and started thinking through other outfit options, but the technician stopped me and grabbed a nearby multitool. He sliced a half-inch off of the short end of his spare hotel key card, then told me how to use this piece to stiffen my dress fabric behind the mic clip, keeping it put. I'm forever indebted to him for teaching me a cool presentation trick and reducing my anxiety before I got onstage to speak.

Power up!

Some events build in a tech or sound check during breaks between talks, before you go on. When you first plug your laptop into the projector or open your slide deck on a shared laptop, click through everything to make sure it works. (If you're plugging in only moments before your talk, you may have to bravely wing it and hope for the best!)

Ask to see the slides on the projector, and verify they look right and are still readable to the audience in the event lighting. If you have presenter notes, ensure you're still able to see them on your laptop screen or nearby monitor. And if the event has a countdown timer, make sure you can see it from where you're standing.

If you have a live demo in your presentation, practice transitioning from your deck to the demo and back again. Confirm internet access; if you choose to tether from your phone, check your cellular coverage. Also test any audio connection if your talk features sound.

Last, click through your slides with your remote (if you have one) to make sure it's connected correctly. Triple-check you have enough power on your laptop to run through the entire presentation, or plug it in—and ensure its screen won't fall asleep midway through your talk.

Don't forget to check your own energy levels. Social psychologist Amy Cuddy says that "power posing" before an important event can affect your body chemistry to boost confidence (https://www.ted.com/talks/amy_cuddy_your_body_language_shapes_who_you_are). You can do these stances backstage, in the bathroom, or even slightly offstage as you wait to go on. I love to "Superman" pose for a minute or two before my talk, and I've had a good laugh with copresenters (laughing also calms stage nerves!) at how ridiculous we look getting ourselves ready.

This is it! Start your engines; let's do this thing!

CHAPTER SEVEN

The talk

WHILE I DOUBT you're blazing through these pages the minute before you step into the spotlight, I hope this chapter can help reassure and prepare you for that moment. For me, that's when the swell of nerves and butterflies and energy kicks in. No matter how many talks I've given, I still get that rush right before I start speaking.

In her excellent article on overcoming stage fright, designer and developer Emily Lewis writes:

> *Once I'm at the venue and attendees are starting to take their seats, my physical response often starts to override my "you are prepared" mantra. It is then that I try to shift focus away from me, because my presentation isn't about me. It's about my topic and the audience. [...] Focusing on my topic reminds me why I'm there: to share and educate, to inspire others to care, and to showcase an important area of a field that I love. (http://ladiesintech.com/overcoming-stage-fright/)*

Let's remember there is tremendous power in being nervous; it means you care deeply about this topic and presenting this information well. Being nervous is normal.

And if none of that relieves the sweat on your palms, know too: standing up onstage is a finite amount of time. You're here to do this one job. Know that the anxiety will pass, whether it's after you deliver your first line or when the last person applauds.

In the meantime, let's walk through a rough timeline of getting onstage, delivering your talk, and *celebrating* afterward.

Is this thing on?

Find ways to cheer yourself on throughout your talk, for both your brain and your body. For example, I like to sneak a sticky note with a simple, happy phrase or the name of someone I love onto my laptop below my keyboard. Whenever I set up my screen or glance at my keyboard to advice a slide or read from my presenter notes, I get a glimpse of that reassuring reminder, smile, and feel a little more relaxed.

I bring these bursts of happiness to my slide deck too—a while ago, I started incorporating pictures of sloths, my go-to animal for total ridiculousness and joy. I sprinkle them throughout my presentation and grin every time I see them. Seeing something you love while onstage is a delightful way to pep yourself up as you speak.

Or try grounding yourself in your surroundings. As you step onto the stage, note to yourself how it feels to be in this light, or how sturdy the floor feels underneath your feet. Feel the weight of the remote in your hand. If it helps, look to the countdown timer during your talk—time *is* passing and you only have to stand here for a set amount of time. There's a light at the end of this tunnel of nerves. If your conference doesn't provide a timer, try the built-in timer in your presentation software or a stopwatch on your phone. (And if staring at a big clock counting down *adds* to your stress, avert your eyes.)

As you stand on the stage, remember: your audience is anticipating you'll be *successful* at giving this talk. To them, everything has been well thought-out and prepared; they walk in assuming (rightly!) they're going to learn something new or be inspired…and you're the person who'll show them how.

Our bodies, ourselves

As someone who gets tongue-tied during those initial moments onstage, I'm here to reassure you it's totally fine if your first line flops. The audience is getting to know you and will forget about it in less than two minutes. They're rooting for your success—they won't remember a minor flub, no matter how awkward it sounds in your head.

A few survey respondents shared how anxiety seems to spring from their bodies, as in: "I have the type of anxiety that just happens—there is no one fear that cripples me, and mentally I am fine until I get up in front of everyone, and then my body takes over."

It's so hard to feel out of sync with one's body. My number-one fear is tripping and falling on my way up the stage. Others worried about needing to use the bathroom during their talk, throwing up, getting a nosebleed, or contracting hiccups.

At the core of these is a concern the audience will assume we, as the speaker, are uncomfortable onstage. We want to look natural, like we have this under control, and we definitely don't want our bodies to give away how we're really feeling—or to operate independently of our mental state.

If any of these body-conscious nerves feel familiar, let me offer this advice: breathe, and remember all your preparation for this moment. If you stumble over your words, take a breath and give yourself a second to recover, then charge on. If you feel yourself blushing (and I'm a frequent stage blusher), breathe, and then refocus on the presentation. If you lose your train of thought, let yourself pause, and then reflect on your presenter notes. Pauses tend to feel longer to a presenter than to an audience; they'll be listening like normal.

As you breathe, remember you have prepared for this talk. You've done the work! You've practiced and revised based on feedback. Now, it's simply your time to perform the job you've come all this way to do.

We can't control our bodies, but we can put in a strong delivery of our presentation, and that's what people will remember.

Reading the audience

Many survey responses revolved around the fear of boring or losing the audience. Delivering a talk is an interactive experience; it makes sense that being able to read the audience is a source of anxiety.

Let's acknowledge it can be difficult to see your audience when you're onstage: the lights are bright, the first row of seats may be far from your laptop (where you'll be directing your attention), and you'll be so concentrated on delivering your content your brain might not have the focus available to read the people in front of you. In this case, give yourself a break and rely on your prep to keep you going strong.

If you *are* at an event where you can see and hear the audience, you may start to develop a sense for how well your talk is going over. This takes time. In my early talks, I didn't hear laughter—not because the crowd was silent, but because I was too nervous and focused on my delivery to notice anything else. These days, I'm able to devote more brain space to reading the room (and registering laughs at my jokes). I can take stock of nods, "ahs" of understanding, and whether people are leaning toward me to listen intently.

Further, after giving the same talk a number of times, I'm able to compare audience reactions to major parts of a story, and use that information to decide if I should riff more or cut to the chase faster. I try to remember what the audience responded to and compare it with tweets and post-talk blog posts from attendees. (Again, this kind of data-gathering takes practice, and I definitely wasn't equipped to clock this kind of peripheral feedback early on.)

But let's back up and return to you. You're onstage, and your audience is just...there. I'll argue that typical audience cues for boredom, like being silent or burying their heads in their laptops or phones, aren't always an indicator you've lost them. I'd go so far to say they could be great signs; quiet people are also focused people, and maybe they're furiously note-taking or tweeting about your talk.

If people walk out of your talk, especially at a multi-track conference, don't take it to heart. They could've simply ended up in the wrong room or needed to duck out to take care of something. Since many events record sessions for later, people might hop around and catch up on your talk afterward. Or maybe, for whatever reason, the audience member isn't into it. And that's okay!

Please hold yourself back from worrying about that audience member leaving while you're onstage. Your goal is to deliver this talk to the people who are *in* the room. You have a finite amount of energy to help get you through; don't spend it on the person who left! If you start spiraling, take a breath and try to pick out a face in the crowd. Focus on that face, glance at your presenter notes or the many other attentive people, and get back into the flow.

If you do lose an audience's attention, you'll learn you have more work to do to iterate on your presentation or delivery style for the next event, *after* you leave the stage. It won't be that helpful to concern yourself with it while you're speaking, unless you have a ton of mental capacity available to deliver your talk *and* read the audience *and* devise a way to get their attention back. More likely, you'll want to prioritize the work of delivering your talk and visit potential ways to improve it after you're done.

Handling Q&A

A question-and-answer session gives the audience a chance to follow up on or clarify points in your talk, ask for more nuanced info to help put your lessons into action, or, frankly, feel more connected to you, the speaker. Hopefully, the question applies to other audience members too, so more people can pick up extra tidbits. In addition to the practice suggestions in Chapter 5, tee up Q&A with clear directions for your audience.

As I transition into Q&A, I'll explicitly say it's time for questions and what the process is to ask one. Every event is different: some events don't have microphones for audience members, some have a mic stand for people to walk up to, and some pass a mic around to people who raise their hands. I'll say something like, "Now it's time to ask questions! Raise your hand and someone will hand you a mic," or "Now we're going to do Q&A! I will repeat questions before answering them so everyone can hear."

Trick(y) questions

Obviously, you want Q&A to be as helpful to as many people as possible. But the goal of Q&A is *not* to make everybody happy, nor is it to teach material irrelevant to the scope of your talk. You get to determine your Q&A and how it goes; you have a lot of power to reframe questions, move on from weird ones, and do whatever you can to help the audience continue to learn.

The most productive questions are open ones, where you can answer in a multitude of ways (and adapt your response to your current audience). Closed questions, on the other hand, require only a "yes" or "no." These tend to be less helpful (and likely easily settled with an online search). Answer these simply. If you can, connect it to an idea or tool that might interest the rest of the crowd. Otherwise, move on.

Sometimes, audience members ask questions that aren't actually questions—which isn't always bad! I've had people say, "Everybody in this audience should read Lara's post on XYZ, because it is great!" (Thanks, buddy!) Other times (oh boy), an audience member might be trying to appear smart. Or start an argument. Or dismiss you based on their experience. This can feel awkward! But recognize this peacocking isn't about you. This person's actions and words are purely a reflection of them and whatever they have going on. Who knows why they feel the need to raise their hand and say words out loud to a large group of people. The important thing is remembering their non-question has little to do with you or the quality of your presentation. Know too the audience is rooting for you, and they want this audience member to stop talking as much as you do. They'd rather go back to learning!

Further, there's no rule you need to accept the premise of a question. You can ask the person to reword ("I'm not sure

I understand. Could you clarify?"), or you can reflect what you heard and ask, "Is that what you mean?" I've also flat-out rephrased questions to ones I'd rather answer, something I think would better benefit the audience to hear. Feel free to reframe questions to make them more digestible or relevant to your topic. When I reframe a question, I'll acknowledge doing so: "I know I answered a slightly different question than the one you asked." And then I smile before moving on.

It's your job to keep the program on track, because you're the one with the microphone and spotlight. You get to set the tone. By reminding yourself the work in a Q&A is to continue to help the audience learn something new and relevant, hopefully you can give yourself permission to circumvent awkward, aggressive, or unhelpful audience responses.

Impostor syndrome

Raise your hand if you've ever calmly conducted a conversation (with a boss, a client, or a coworker) while internally chanting, "I don't know what I'm doing!" If so, you're not alone. Many of us—and many survey respondents—have felt like imposters at some point in our careers. We worry we don't know as much as we think we do or we don't really deserve to be onstage sharing our expertise.

This feeling is hard to shake. Some doubt is normal, and can even be a good sign—see the Dunning-Kruger effect (http://citeseerx.ist.psu.edu/viewdoc/download?doi=10.1.1.64.2655&rep=rep1&type=pdf, PDF). More important, remember why you have airtime at this event: you are passionate about this subject, and the event organizers wanted folks to hear about it from you. No one knows all there is to know on any topic; if someone asks a question you don't know the answer to, it doesn't mean you don't know *anything*. (You might revisit the tips in Chapter 5.)

If an audience member points out something you have no clue about, great! You just learned something new, and given this is a topic you're excited about, you're probably eager to pick up that new skill. One time during Q&A, an audience member ran an impromptu experiment based on an idea he'd had during my presentation, and raised his hand to share the results with everyone. His approach was *super cool* and gave us something different to try that totally worked. I was delighted, thanked him, and asked him to tweet about it. This moment wasn't about revealing a gap in my knowledge. In fact, it's a fast-forward to what you hope your audience does after the talk: take what you give them, and build something awesome.

On harassment

For some, thinking about unruly or antagonistic audience members escalates into a much bigger (and valid) concern. A number of survey respondents mentioned fears of harassment during or after giving a talk:

- "Saying something that brings down the wrath of the internet-hate-mob."
- "Becoming a target for harassment."
- "[Experiencing] backlash afterward. Doxxing or releasing personal information about me/my family."

In the wake of events like GamerGate, those expressed fears (with which I identify) are very real. If you're concerned about being harassed as a public speaker, you might consider a few mitigation tactics to hopefully make you feel more comfortable. For instance, choose events with a Code of Conduct that organizers are prepared to enforce. Ask them how they plan to deal with harassers. These conversations will also help you feel out who on staff you can talk to about any issues during or after the event. Another resource is Feminist Frequency's "Speak Up & Stay Safe(r): A Guide to Protecting Yourself From Online Harassment" (https://onlinesafety.feministfrequency.com/en/). The website suggests harassment-prevention measures, like improving the security of your passwords and removing your personally identifiable information from public view.

If you experience harassment while at the event, follow the steps in the Code of Conduct (if it exists), such as contacting the designated person to help. Be sure to prioritize your safety and health; remember that being in shock, or feeling unable to directly address harassment yourself, is perfectly normal. As possible, lean on the event staff and those around you, and consult resources like the Geek Feminism Wiki, which lists strategies to consider when reporting harassment (http:// geekfeminism.wikia.com/wiki/Reporting_harassment).

The act of public speaking is incredibly courageous. You are choosing to go and be vulnerable onstage, under a spotlight, in front of a group of people. But you're choosing to do so because your voice and your topic are important to share.

After the talk

Let out that breath, give a cheer—and ride that adrenaline high! Your primary work is done: you delivered your talk, maybe you answered some questions, and now it's time to applaud yourself.

Do what you please: some people enjoy celebrating with others, some want to be alone for a while and decompress. I personally love holing up in a quiet place where no one can find me for an hour or so after a talk; it gives me time to think on how it went and see if people shared their impressions online yet.

Collect feedback

Gather external sources of feedback to check how well your content resonated with the audience and how you might improve your presentation for next time.

I like to start with Twitter to see which parts of the talk were quoted—it gives me a sense of what appealed most to folks, and I'll consider going deeper into those aspects if I give the presentation again. I also note which parts people *didn't* talk about or link to, and I'll consider if I should try a different tack or discard it, or (if it's fundamental to the talk) keep it as is.

I also check:

- Clicks on the custom bit.ly links I've built into the slides or resources page. Which tools or articles in particular were people interested in seeing for themselves?

- Overall visits to the resources page and the SpeakerDeck version of the slides.
- Star ratings on the conference website for the talk, if such functionality exists. Some event organizers provide feedback directly to the speaker after the event, based on audience surveys or general conversations.

Public feedback can be exhilarating and daunting. As you log people's reactions, try to focus on the constructive pieces (Chapter 5's diamonds and spades!)—the notes that'll make your talk even stronger for the future. Bask in all the praise. If you see feedback criticizing you as a person, policing your tone, or otherwise providing unhelpful advice, chuck it in the garbage. As engineering manager Raquel Vélez reminds us, "Talks don't define you; *you* define you. Talks come and go, but every single one will make you a better you" (https://twitter.com/rockbot/status/661281974246477824).

Check in with yourself

Complement others' feedback with your own assessment. Ask yourself: How did that go? What did I notice most during the talk? How do I feel? What would I want to do next time?

Tracking these questions will help you hone your instincts as a speaker. For starters, try stacking your answers against audience responses, and see where they differ or overlap. Maybe your brain is still stuck on a mistake you made, but no one has made a fuss about it. Or perhaps you spent extra time going deep into a technical detail in Q&A, based on a gut-check of audience interest—and your explanation is repeatedly quoted.

Your answers will help you weigh the feedback you receive, but more crucial, they give you the chance to express how well your talk worked for *you*. (You might revisit your initial goals for speaking, from way back in Chapter 1.) If you can stomach it, watch the recording of your presentation to see how you did. Or give the same talk again, in a different venue, and start to learn how different events and audiences respond to you. Each talk is a chance to shape your content, your delivery, your persona into whatever makes you excited to take the stage; this exercise of checking in with yourself is a springboard for you to decide what you'd like to practice next.

When it comes to improving, remember we can't get better at everything all at once. So what's the one thing you want to work on for next time? Maybe when you watch the video, you notice you'd like to take more pauses or do something else with your hands. Or maybe you feel you didn't have a good read on the audience, so you brainstorm ways to build in more interactions, like asking attendees more questions or simply reminding yourself to look up from your presenter notes.

We can all improve our game by practicing, reflecting, and learning from others—and ourselves.

Celebrate your achievement

After my talk is done, after I've answered questions, checked the data, and thanked people, I'll go find a donut.

Years ago, whenever I achieved something—like giving a talk—I wouldn't take the time to celebrate it, because the feeling of success was so intangible. It's not like you're sauntering from the venue, boosting a trophy; it's all too easy to keep zooming forward, never acknowledging to yourself the big-deal thing you did. And because I skipped out on noting each real and hard-earned (how much of this book is about preparation?) achievement, I felt like I wasn't moving toward my goals.

To combat this feeling, I decided to be deliberate about marking accomplishments by eating one donut—sitting down, savoring it, and spending a few minutes thinking about the work I put in. Carving out a moment to celebrate lets me really *feel* like I did something; it's a delicious and tangible reminder I've accomplished an otherwise-intangible career goal.

Throughout this book, I hope you've been able to identify your fears about public speaking and address them in ways that feel comfortable to you. Wrestling with worries, making plans forward—these deserve whatever your version of a donut is. Mark down this moment. You've put in time and tremendous effort. Revel in it.

Acknowledgements

First, I'd like to thank the women behind Technically Speaking, Chiu-Ki Chan and Cate Huston, and the founder of Ladies in Tech, Jenn Lukas. A *ton* of links, quotes, and other ideas shared in this book originally sprang from these resources.

This book was shaped by these phenomenal feedback-givers: Rachel Andrew, Juan Pablo Buriticá, Karyn Campbell, Anna Debenham, Jenn Downs, Elizabeth Ferrao, Shawn Hogan, Cate Huston, Jeremy Keith, Meri Williams, Maggie Zhou, and my editor, Tina Lee. Thank you each for your thoughtfulness and words of wisdom.

Thanks and a big hug to Zane, Adam, Paloma, and Mike for letting me write the book from their heavenly houses, next to their snuggly pups. Their love and homes welcomed and nurtured me in a multitude of ways, and I'm eternally grateful. To my mentor and cheerleader Daniel—I'm honored to be your friend. Thanks for your encouragement, allyship, and coffee.

Thanks especially to my family, and to those who have become like family: Masha, coach Jen, Jason, and my teammates. I absolutely could not have done this without your support, and I feel incredibly lucky to know you and have you in my corner. To the badass women in tech who help me through: thank you.

All of my love to Lauren Sperber. For her patience, smarts, critical feedback, sarcasm, and seemingly endless support. A million donuts to her.

Resources

- Technically Speaking, a newsletter by Chiu-Ki Chan and Cate Huston, delivers calls for proposals (CFPs), speaking tips, and inspirational videos straight to your inbox (https://tinyletter.com/techspeak).
- Ladies in Tech, a collection of articles and resources curated by Jenn Lukas, serves to help and encourage women to speak at tech conferences (http://ladiesintech.com/).
- "How to Prepare and Write a Tech Conference Talk," an article by Lena Reinhard, covers her entire topic selection and talk preparation process (http://wunder.schoenaberselten.com/2016/02/16/how-to-prepare-and-write-a-tech-conference-talk/).
- "How to Become a Public Speaker in 1 Year—Step 1: Build Confidence" is the first article in an excellent series by Catt Small about getting to that event stage (https://medium.com/@cattsmall/how-to-become-a-public-speaker-in-1-year-step-1-build-confidence-253aa61b4d52#.6f2hj64yd).

Talk Proposals

Here are some tips from experienced speakers and event organizers on choosing a talk topic and drafting a proposal.

- "Ignite—I Have Nothing to Say," Chiu-Ki Chan, https://www.youtube.com/watch?v=MLdhamQlFfg
- "My Process: Writing a Talk," Camille Fournier, https://medium.com/@skamille/my-process-writing-a-talk-de55a870f2e7
- "A Process for Writing an Abstract," Cate Huston, http://www.catehuston.com/blog/2015/11/27/a-process-for-writing-an-abstract/
- "What Your Conference Proposal Is Missing," Sarah Mei, http://www.sarahmei.com/blog/2014/04/07/what-your-conference-proposal-is-missing/
- "Finding Your Killer Talk Idea," Rachel Nabors, http://ladiesintech.com/finding-your-killer-talk-idea/

- "Conference Prompts: Or How to Submit Proposals and Influence People," Noel Rappin, http://www.noelrappin.com/railsrx/2014/1/18/conference-prompts-or-how-to-submit-proposals-and-influence-people
- "What I Learned from Reading 429 Conference Proposals," Noel Rappin, http://www.noelrappin.com/railsrx/2014/3/17/what-i-learned-from-reading-429-conference-proposals
- "You Have to Ask to Get a Yes," Estelle Weyl, http://ladiesintech.com/you-have-to-ask-to-get-a-yes/
- Topic Generation Worksheet, WriteSpeakCode, https://github.com/WriteSpeakCode/2013curriculum/blob/master/speak/WSC2013_Speak_TopicGenerationWorksheet.pdf

Talk Structure and Content

Ready to start shaping your topic into a talk? Use these resources to develop your narrative and craft your slides.

- "The Simple Trick to Avoid Overwhelming Your Audience," Leslie Belknap, https://blog.slideshare.net/2015/10/26/the-simple-trick-to-avoid-overwhelming-your-audience
- "Storyforming," Jeremy Keith, https://adactio.com/journal/9732
- "On Choosing a Syntax Highlighting Scheme for Your Next Presentation," Rebecca Murphey, http://rmurphey.com/blog/2012/11/29/choosing-presentation-color-scheme
- *Show and Tell: How Everybody Can Make Extraordinary Presentations*, Dan Roam, http://www.danroam.com/show-tell/
- "So, You've Been Invited to Speak," Lea Verou, http://lea.verou.me/2012/06/so-youve-been-invited-to-speak/

Preparing for and Delivering the Talk

Lean on these tips from experienced speakers to pack, travel, and mentally prepare yourself for the spotlight.
- "The Itinerant Geek," Rachel Andrew, http://alistapart.com/article/the-itinerant-geek

- "Your Body Language Shapes Who You Are," Amy Cuddy, https://www.ted.com/talks/amy_cuddy_your_body_language_shapes_who_you_are
- "Returning to the Stage... After Harassment," Cate Huston, http://www.catehuston.com/blog/2014/04/30/returning-to-the-stage-after-harrassment/
- "The Speakers' Checklist," Emma Jane, http://trainingintheopen.com/speakers-checklist.html

Index

Colophon

The text is set in Lora, by Cyreal, and Lato, by Łukasz Dziedzic.

 This book was printed in the United States using FSC certified papers.

About the Author

 **Lara Callender Hogan** is an engineering director at Etsy and the author of *Designing for Performance* (O'Reilly, 2014) and the coauthor of *Building a Device Lab* (Five Simple Steps, 2015).

In her world tour to advocate web performance to designers and developers alike, Lara has presented at Google I/O, keynoted the Velocity Conference, and given talks at organizations like the New York Times and the Hillary Clinton campaign. To connect her work with her activism, Lara donates proceeds from *Designing for Performance* to charities focused on supporting underrepresented people in tech.

Lara also believes it's important to celebrate career achievements with donuts.

www.ingramcontent.com/pod-product-compliance
Lightning Source LLC
Chambersburg PA
CBHW040155160726
48006CB00014B/1759